Whose Body Is It?

The troubling issue of
informed consent

Carolyn Faulder

Published by VIRAGO PRESS Limited 1985
41 William IV Street, London WC2

Reprinted 1985

British Library Cataloguing in Publication Data
Faulder, Carolyn
    Whose body is it?
    1. Sick—Legal status, law etc.—Great
    Britain   2. Great Britain—National
    Health Service
    I.   Title
    362.1'0941   KD3395

ISBN 0–86068–645–0

Typeset by Folio Photosetting, Bristol
Printed in Great Britain by litho at
Anchor Brendon, Tiptree, Essex

To John – thank you for listening, encouraging and enduring

Contents

Acknowledgements   ix

Introduction   1

Part one   Respect for persons

1   Informed consent – what are we talking about?   9
Origins and a brief look at American case law

2   Informed consent – the right to know   16
Principles, values and rights
Health rights
Moral and legal rights
Feelings are not enough
The five principles

3   Understanding consent – the right to say no   32
Sorting out the semantics
The reasonable person
Exceptions
True informed consent

4   Codes and laws   44
Hippocrates at Helsinki
Protection or defence?

Part two   Limits to science

5   Randomised controlled clinical trials   61
The scientific art
Human experimentation
Planning the protocol
Running a randomised controlled trial (RCT)
Why randomise?
Pitfalls and problems

6   Trials on trial   75
Are they ethical?
Variations on randomisation
Alternatives to randomisation
Are placebos ethical?
When to stop and other problems for doctors

7   In whose hands?   95
Who decides?
Who pays?

Part three   Changing the perspective

8   Dilemmas for doctors   109
A principle and its practice
The communication gap
Obtaining consent
Explaining randomisation
Paternalism – is there a case for it?

9   Whose body is it?   121
The politics of contempt
A Patient's Bill of Rights
No rights without responsibilities

Appendix A   130

Appendix B   137

Appendix C   141

Chapter references   143

Select bibliography   148

Index   150

Acknowledgements

This book could not have been written without the support and help of innumerable people: those who were so generous with their time and knowledge and pointed me down many avenues of research; patients and ex-patients who gave me the inestimable benefit of their personal experiences and views; my medical friends, in particular those on the Cancer Research Campaign Working Party in Breast Conservation with whom I have spent many constructive and enlightening hours exploring the issue of informed consent; fellow members of the Society of Applied Philosophy whose insights and comments which emerged from our discussions in the medical workshops were immeasurably useful.

Special thanks are due to the following: Professor Michael Baum who first alerted me to the importance of informed consent; Dr Maureen Roberts who read the book when it was in preparation and gave me invaluable comments and criticisms; Dr Jeffrey Tobias who enabled me to use the resources of the library at the Royal Society of Medicine; Professor Ian Kennedy who gave me the same facility at King's College Centre of Law, Medicine and Ethics; Gillian Barnard and her colleagues at the Marylebone Medical Library who were endlessly patient in seeking out and photocopying references for me; Nef Jandu and John Parker who voluntarily appointed themselves as my legal scouts and drew my attention to reports and papers I would otherwise certainly have missed; Bob Brecher for our extended discussion about autonomy; Ruthie Petrie for her sympathetic editing; Ursula Owen and Jacqueline Korn who encouraged me to believe this was a book worth writing.

Its faults and deficiencies are of course entirely my responsibility.

Introduction

Should patients be fully involved in making decisions about their treatment? How much should patients be told about the risks and benefits attaching to a particular treatment? Should doctors inform patients about alternative treatments? Why is it that so many patients do not know that they have been entered into a clinical trial which is comparing alternative treatments? What are clinical trials and how are they planned and run? What do patients really want to know? How much responsibility do they want to take for their own bodies? Are doctors right in assuming that most patients prefer to leave the difficult decisions to them?

These are all questions we may start asking only when we experience medical treatment for ourselves or find that we are living through a serious illness with someone who is close to us. Central to them all is the concept of 'the doctrine of informed consent' which, in recent years, has become the subject of considerable soul-searching and debate within the medical profession, yet it remains largely unfamiliar to the general public. I believe we should be exploring the ethical and medical issues the doctrine raises now, in our capacity as health-care consumers, rather than waiting until we become patients. That is why I have written this book – to open up the debate and bring it into the public arena where it rightly belongs.

Although I do not intend to suggest that there has been a deliberate conspiracy among doctors to hush up public discussion about

informed consent, I do think that the profession in general is unduly
nervous about exposing its doubts and worries to public scrutiny. But
the public is us and the public is the society in which we live.
Professionals and lay people alike, we are all members of the same
society and we therefore share a common responsibility to thrash out
the ever-increasing range of ethical problems which are now being
presented to us by recent astonishing scientific advances, especially in
the field of biomedical technology. If we believe that the decisions
doctors make about our bodies ought to be our decisions too, then it is
high time for us to take a more positive, active and informed role in
that process.

It seems extraordinary that while informed consent has become a
crucial issue in medical ethics, few of us – and that includes doctors –
can honestly claim to have a clear idea of what we really mean by it, or
when and in what medical situations we, as patients, can reasonably
expect to be asked to give it. Informed consent lacks the dramatic
headline appeal of so many other current ethical concerns in medicine
such as surrogate motherhood or research on embryos, but we should
not be lulled into thinking that it is therefore less important. Informed
consent is about the right to control our own destinies and to
determine our own ends as far as is humanly possible; it is about the
right to make choices and the right to refuse consent; it is about the
right of individuals to preserve their integrity and dignity whatever
physical and mental deterioration they may suffer through ill health; it
is about our duty always and in all circumstances to respect each other
as fellow human beings and as persons.

Far from being a matter of subsidiary interest, I maintain that
informed consent is *the* ethical issue in medicine today and that unless
we sort out our views and determine what we really mean when we
talk about the patient's right to give informed consent, we are
imperilling our ability to make wise and humane decisions about all
the other bioethical problems now facing us. I say this, well aware that
many people, including even some of the ethicists and doctors who
are most concerned about the prevailing lack of informed consent,
particularly in clinical trials, will think I am over-stating the case. Even
if I cannot convince the sceptics and the doubters by argument, I hope
that the examples I cite of trials which, by any standard – moral,
medical or scientific – should never have been allowed, will persuade
them that the price we pay for ignoring this right is too high. In the

rating table of human values, I believe that striving to retain our moral integrity must always score higher than our quest for knowledge or our scientific achievements.

This book is part enquiry, part a personal statement of my views about the meaning of informed consent and its relevance for patients and doctors, especially in the context of randomised controlled clinical trials. As such I have found it necessary to examine in some depth the serious ethical issues which arise from the trials themselves. There are no precise data available to say how many patients are entered into trials, but an informed guessestimate suggests about 10 per cent of the total patient population. Although small proportionately, this is nonetheless a significant figure, especially when we consider how much weight and importance doctors attach to the results rendered by these trials.

I am keenly conscious, however, that in concentrating on this particular aspect of informed consent I have touched only peripherally on other areas of medical behaviour in which it is just as necessary to seek the patient's knowledgeable involvement. Specifically, there is the vitally important matter of preserving patient confidentiality which is becoming increasingly threatened by two things: on the one hand, the scientific concern to share and disseminate information which, on the other, is aided and abetted by advancing computerisation. I hope that I will not be regarded as evading the issue when I say that the subject is so complex it needs a book to itself. Quite definitely, it needs a vigorous and informed input from the public, and never more urgently than now when the Data Protection Bill is going through its Parliamentary stages. At this point I am prepared to state boldly that those readers who find themselves sharing my conviction that it is essential to insist on their right to informed consent will find that all the arguments I produce to support this contention apply with equal force to the issue of confidentiality.

I must confess that when I embarked on this book I felt rather as I imagine a learner parachutist must feel as he or she contemplates the first jump from an aeroplane – a heady blend of terror and anticipation. First let me explain my misgivings. I am neither doctor, philosopher, scientist nor lawyer, yet informed consent is a complex subject which ramifies into all these specialist areas. To some extent this explains why the debate about informed consent has hitherto been largely confined to esoteric journals and books in which it is discussed in a manner which makes no concession to the uninitiated outsider. The arguments both for and against informed consent are riddled with technicalities and wrapped up in tortuous experts' jargon which means we have to pick them apart carefully before we can begin to comprehend their basic meaning. These barriers to understanding are entirely man-made (I use the term advisedly because the number of women specialists in any of these areas who have written on the subject can be counted on the fingers of one hand, as the references and bibliography testify), but I think we should regard them as providing a challenge to meet and overcome rather than as an insuperable obstacle.

My sole credentials for leaping so recklessly, some will certainly say, presumptuously, into this dangerous void are these: I work as a journalist; I have been a patient and will probably be one again one of these days – it is a fate few escape; finally, I am a feminist. They are, I believe, qualifications enough to dare to breach the defences of expert opinion and to encourage my lay readers to come with me. As a journalist I am committed to seeking information and to trying to clarify the needlessly obscure, especially when it concerns subjects of great general interest which should and must be widely understood. My experiences of being a hospitalised patient, although relatively brief and untraumatic, taught me, as many others will also have learned, how hard it is to retain a sense of identity and firm purpose when one is caught up in the medical machine. My feminist convictions have made me realise that women will never be in control of their lives until they take charge of their bodies.

The seeking and giving of informed consent in a medical context applies equally, of course, to men as to women, but there is no doubt that female patients are more at risk of having their wishes disregarded, because the medical profession is so excessively paternalistic and male dominated. Clichés these terms may have become, but this does not diminish their essential relevance. Women, because of their reproductive life cycle, tend to be at the receiving end of medical care and attention from an earlier age and for much more of their lives than are men. Their encounters with doctors are frequently fraught with sexual prejudice. Women who are patients or the mothers of sick children often find extreme difficulty in persuading doctors to take their complaints seriously: at one level they may walk into their GP's surgery with a request for help in discovering the source of genuine pain or in coping with severe depression, only to find themselves being sent on their way with a prescription for Valium and a few ill-chosen platitudes ringing in their ears; at another they may be chided or patronised for indulging in what the doctor chooses to regard as foolish or misplaced fears. I do not intend to suggest that this happens all the time, or only to women. There are many admirable doctors who are prepared to spend considerable time with all their patients and who have trained themselves to listen, observe and ask pertinent questions as an inseparable part of their diagnostic procedure. Equally, the old-fashioned medical paternalist is not particularly discriminating about who he – and it is usually 'he' – puts down. However well-intentioned the purpose, however kindly the manner, the effect is usually intimidating, more especially if the patient happens to be elderly, working class or inarticulate, or all three combined.

Many times I have been told with some impatience by doctors that it is one thing for the 'educated' middle classes to insist on their rights, quite another to think that the vast majority of patients either want to be fully informed or expect their doctors to be anything other than all knowing and magisterially benevolent. This attitude seems to me to betray an insulting contempt for the intelligence and self-awareness of the average patient. We may not always be able to formulate the 'proper' questions or express our personal wishes as decisively and clearly as we would like; nonetheless, we may know at least as well as our doctors what those needs are and can certainly guess when we are being denied information which we would consider important for ourselves. And anyway, who of us is at our best or most lucid when feeling wretched in a hospital bed and probably stuffed full of drugs and tubes to boot?

The cause I plead in this book – the right of patients to have their autonomy respected and their human dignity protected in sickness as in health – is a humanist cause. As such it embraces and extends the meaning of feminism as I understand it – the conviction that women and men are equal human beings who owe each other equality of respect and consideration. It is a cause grounded in respect for persons, regardless of their age, sex, class, or race, and it is a cause confirmed by ethical principles which our society has come to accept as fundamentally valuable, whether or not we deviate from them, individually or *en masse*.

There is, of course, no point in paying lipservice to high-sounding moral sentiments if they seem in some way to be alien to common sense or so impossibly idealistic that we cannot hope to live up to them. That is why, at the risk of being accused of pedantry, I ask the reader to bear with me and to follow me patiently through the network of philosophical arguments, the legal niceties ('nasties' might be a more apt term), the scientific aims and procedures of clinical trials, the ethical difficulties these trials introduce and the psychological constraints they impose and, finally, some of the practical solutions we could be considering for making real headway towards the goal of informed consent. My aim has been to simplify without, I hope, becoming simplistic. In no way do I pretend to have come up with final answers, but I hope that readers who join me in exploring this problematic ethical issue, which affects us all at some point in our lives, will agree that it is a matter which demands our commitment and our response.

A NOTE ABOUT REFERENCES AND TERMINOLOGY

It has not been my intention to write yet another academic treatise. I have, however, drawn on an extensive literature to which some readers will wish to refer. In order to avoid the tedium of too many footnotes encumbering the text, I have cited specific references at the bottom of the page only when I have thought it necessary for clarity. The Chapter references contain further source material relating to each chapter and these, of course, are also copiously furnished with still more references for those who are studiously inclined. The general reader will probably be more interested in the books recommended in the Select bibliography.

I make no apology for my solution to the perennial problem of sexist designation in our English language. Wherever an alternative seemed too clumsy, the feminine gender has been ascribed to patients and the masculine to doctors. It is after all unarguable that most medical scientists and specialists are male and that most of the patients in the trials which I mention are female.

Part one
Respect for persons

Act in such a way that you treat humanity, both in your own person and in the person of all others, never as a means but always equally as an end.

Immanuel Kant, *Groundwork of the Metaphysics of Morals*

1 Informed consent – what are we talking about?

> As a doctrine and as a practical reality, informed consent is neither so complicated nor so difficult as doctors and lawyers would make it, nor is there any good reason for the extended medical debates it engenders. At its core, it is respect for the patient as an individual, not a defense against the possibility of a later malpractice suit.
>
> Jory Graham, *In the Company of Others*

In August 1981, an eighty-three-year-old widow, Mrs Margaret Wigley, following an operation for bowel cancer, was entered into a randomised controlled clinical trial to test a new drug. She was not told that she was in a trial, nor did she know that the treatment she was getting was experimental. No one asked her to give her informed consent.

Two weeks later she died because her bone marrow had become irreversibly depressed owing to careless monitoring of the effects of the drug. If this had not occurred she could certainly have expected to live some months, possibly years more. Before her operation Mrs Wigley was leading an active, independent life. She was not senile and she and her two daughters apparently knew that she had cancer.

At the inquest in July 1982, the coroner, Dr Richard Whittington, expressed his concern on two points: first, that the trial protocol had not been strictly observed (see chapter 5 for a full explanation of what this means); and second, that the patient's consent had not been sought. No fewer than eleven hospital ethical committees had accepted the trial and agreed that the informed consent of patients was not required. Dr Whittington urged that 'the whole idea of concealed controlled trials [should] be brought to the public notice for proper discussion'.

Although this case fomented a good deal of discussion in the medical and legal journals, the national press paid no more than passing attention to the affair. And there the matter rests. The patient is dead, and presumably the relatives felt that they had been through enough without further subjecting themselves to the extended torture and uncertain outcome of taking legal action.

In July 1984, Mr Peter Holtom, a cancer patient with only weeks to live, announced his intention of suing the surgeon for not revealing to him, before operating, that he suspected he had irreversible cancer. Had he known this, said Mr Holtom, he would not have agreed to the operation. More fundamentally, he objected to the doctor taking this decision without consulting him. 'The doctor's view of what are my best interests are not the same as my own view of my best interests and he had no right to make this assumption,' he said in a television interview. 'By doing so he has deprived me of the right to make the decisions I need to make for myself and my family.'

Doctors are not legally obliged to tell patients the truth about their prognosis. If Mr Holtom succeeds in his case and forces doctors in future to tell those patients, who ask to know, that they have no chance of recovery, he will be making legal history. He himself will never know the outcome as he will be dead long before the case comes to court.

Thousands of patients are being entered into clinical trials without their knowledge. Similarly, there are many patients like Mr Holtom who, ask as they will, are met with evasive answers or downright lies about their true condition. Where trials are concerned, doctors justify their behaviour by saying that patients find it difficult to understand the scientific reasons for the study and that their confidence will be undermined if their doctor has to confess that he does not know which treatment is best, hence the need for the trial. As for the dying patient, the doctors' usual answer is that most patients, even those who insist that they do want the unvarnished truth, don't really understand the full implications of what they are asking and that to know the facts would destroy their hope and morale at a time when they need everything they can hold on to just to get them through their last weeks.

Are the doctors right? Or is this a scandal which must not be allowed to continue? Should we not be demanding to know about medical research and the decisions it involves, especially when there is a possibility that we could be unwitting participants in a trial about whose aims, risks and benefits we know nothing? This comment from the author of the section on 'Consent' in the *Dictionary of Medical Ethics* (p. 117) surpasses anything I have met in the medical literature for smug effrontery: 'It is remarkable that there has been no legal action in Great Britain by anyone who thought that research had been done on him without consent, and this may be a tribute to the high ethical standards which have been maintained in the country.'

How can there be action if people do not know that they may have cause for action? By what authority do doctors make up our minds for us? And anyway, whose body is it? The theme of this book is about the patient's right to know, and the patient's right to say no. But to understand what we are demanding we must first understand what we mean when we talk about informed consent.

ORIGINS AND A BRIEF LOOK AT AMERICAN CASE LAW

Most people, if asked what they think is meant by the 'doctrine of informed consent', will look blank and suggest that you tell them. If prompted a little further by the hint that it is related to medical practice, they will probably mention the consent form, usually a brief and minimally informative document which a patient has to sign before an operation. And there they stop. The expression 'informed consent' simply has no place in our current vernacular because the concept itself is almost wholly unfamiliar outside the closed circles of medicine, law and moral philosophy.

Yet ask the same question of any doctor, nurse, medical researcher or other health professional and you will be met by a variety of confusing and confused reactions: dismay, concern, defensiveness and, occasionally, a barely concealed anger that you, a lay person, are intruding into an area of professional behaviour which is really none of your business. Persist, and you will be surprised by the diversity of interpretations which is offered to you. These can range from the nervously uttered statement that 'informed consent means telling patients everything about their condition and leaving the choice of treatment to them' to the dismissive assertion that 'informed consent is a nonsense because patients can't understand all that they are told and shouldn't be allowed to make decisions for themselves'.

Between these two extremes there are vast numbers of conscientious doctors (the majority I would guess) who agonise daily about how much information they should be giving to their patients, in what way they should be communicating, and whether, if they involve their patients in the onerous decision-making process, they may not be making things worse rather than better for them. The doctor's first duty is, after all, to act always in the best interests of the patient. It is how those best interests are interpreted and whose opinion prevails which is the crux of the problem.

Since the medical profession is so divided within itself as to the meaning and purpose of informed consent and is, at the same time, extremely reluctant to confess to its perplexity beyond the confines of professional journals and internal discussions among colleagues, it is hardly surprising that the general British public is profoundly ignorant about the issue. The qualification 'British' is significant, because in both the United States of America and Canada the lay public is far more aware of its rights in this respect. This is in part the result of the many law suits which have been brought and won in the last twenty-five years in which lack of informed consent has been successfully invoked as a ground for negligence. The doctrine has now been officially enshrined in US Federal law.

By contrast, the few judgements that have been made in the British courts during the same period state in essence that the doctrine of informed consent has no legal clout when applied to a medical context – it must remain confined to the narrow field of property rights. The legal position in Britain today is examined in more detail in chapter 4, so at this stage I will note only that orthodox legal opinion is not supported by the entirety of the British legal profession. Even if Mr Holtom's case fails, the matter will not, I suspect, rest there. More attempts will be made to reverse the current situation.

The notion of informed consent is comparatively recent in the history of medical ethics. Indeed, it emerged as a formally stated principle only after the Second World War, following the trial of the Nazi war criminals, most of them doctors, whose appalling experiments on concentration camp inmates in the name of scientific research shocked the world and produced the Nuremberg Code. This code formulates certain basic principles for medical experimentation on human beings, the first of which declares thet 'the voluntary consent of the human subject is absolutely essential' (see Appendix A).

In the intervening years the concept of informed consent has been extended to include medical treatment generally, that is to say clinical practice as well as clinical research, and it has been formalised in a succession of North American legal judgements. In 1960 it was first spelled out in a landmark opinion by the Supreme Court of Kansas when the judge stated:

> Anglo-American law starts with the premise of thorough-going self-determination. It follows that each man is considered to be master of his body, and he may, if he be of sound mind, expressly prohibit the performance of life-saving surgery, or other medical treatment. A doctor might well believe that an operation or form of treatment is desirable or necessary but the law does not permit him to substitute his own judgement for that of the patient by any form of artifice or deception.
>
> (*Natanson* v. *Kline*, Kansas 1960)

Three years later this opinion was endorsed with qualifications in yet another Kansas case, *Williams* v. *Menehan*, Kansas 1963. Here the patient sued for non-disclosure of risks. She had suffered severe burns from radiation therapy following a bilateral mastectomy (the removal of both breasts) for breast cancer. The court stated that the doctor's duty to disclose comprised making 'a reasonable disclosure to his patient of the nature and probable consequences of the suggested or recommended treatment and [making] a knowledgeable disclosure of the dangers within his knowledge which are incident or possible in the treatment he proposes.' The judgement emphasised, however, that the doctor was not obliged to disclose 'all facts, diagnoses and alternatives or possibilities which might occur to [him]' if there was a danger of causing the patient unnecessary anguish.

Being informed about risks is not the same as being told about alternatives to the treatment proposed, and few cases have been brought for failure to disclose any such alternatives that might exist. However, in yet another landmark case (*Canterbury* v. *Spence*, Federal Republic 1972) which was brought by a patient who suffered paralysis following a laminectomy (spinal operation to excise posterior arch of a vertebra), two highly significant principles were asserted. The first was stated thus:

> We reject the thought that the patient should ask for information before the physician is required to disclose. Caveat emptor is not the norm for the consumer of medical services. Duty to disclose is more than a call to speak merely on the patient's request or merely to

answer the patient's questions: it is a duty to volunteer, if necessary, the information the patient needs for intelligent decision.

In short the doctor has a duty to take the initiative in supplying the patient with all the information which she might reasonably consider necessary to assist her in coming to a decision.

The second principle is in a way a development of the first but it also introduces a new consideration since it broaches the all-important question of whose standard should prevail – the patient's or the doctor's. The court's judgement came down unequivocally on the side of the patient in stating that:

> ... to bind the disclosure obligation to medical usage is to arrogate the decision on revelation to the physician alone. Respect for the patient's right to self-determination on particular therapy demands a standard set by law for physicians rather than one which physicians may or may not impose on themselves.

As can be well imagined, these principles taste like very bad medicine indeed to many members of the medical profession, but they have been accepted, in Canada as well as the United States. In 1979 the State of Massachusetts went a step further by pioneering the cause of patients' rights and how they are to be safeguarded. With regard to informed consent it states that 'every patient ... shall be provided by the physician [with] the right ... to informed consent' and *'in the case of a patient suffering from any form of breast cancer, to complete information on all alternative treatments which are medically viable'*. This highly important final injunction is now being adopted by other states. Its significance will not be lost on British readers for whom no such safeguard exists either in the law or in the medical profession's own codes.

I have quoted these American definitions of informed consent at some length because although they do not apply in this country they do offer us a useful reference point for understanding what is meant by the concept. They also show an interesting progression in favour of putting the patient's interests first. There is, however, a serious weakness in making piecemeal decisions on an important principle by a series of legal actions. Instead of providing doctors straight out with a clearly formulated standard to observe, we are dependent on finding a victim willing to sue each time a new point comes up for testing, thus leading us into the morass of defensive medicine, now so rife in the United States, which is proving highly detrimental to doctors and patients alike.

So where does this leave the general public which is you, me, and every other woman and man on the Clapham omnibus? Potential patients every one of us, surely we should be included in the debate about an issue so closely affecting our personal well-being? But we cannot be included if we are vague about the principles at stake and uninformed about the material circumstances to which they apply. As well as examining the meaning of informed consent, we must also consider the nature of the right that we are claiming and the grounds on which we justify our claim that it is the doctor's duty to seek his patient's informed consent. Our arguments must be strong enough to show that informed consent is a matter of ethical principle, not a legal formula or a courtesy which the doctor may or may not extend to his patients as he thinks fit and only to those he deems capable of acting upon it. Furthermore, those arguments must be good enough to convince us, just as definitively as our doctors, that the decision whether to give, or refuse, informed consent always rests with the patient.

2 Informed consent – the right to know

> Learning to understand, accept, and be responsible for
> our physical selves, we . . . can start to use our
> untapped energies. Our image of ourselves is on a
> firmer base, we can be better friends and better lovers,
> better *people*, more self-confident, more autonomous,
> stronger, and more whole.
>
> (Boston Women's Health Book Collective,
> *Our Bodies Ourselves*)

PRINCIPLES, VALUES AND RIGHTS

Statements of ethical principle do not spring out of thin air. They
have their roots in a common human consciousness of something
we call morality, which we believe to be good and to offer a code
of behaviour. The deontologist (derived from the Greek *deon*,
meaning duty) believes that moral principles are absolute and that
they impose an absolute duty on us to obey them. Theologians
and moral philosophers who take this view have constructed
elaborate moral systems which they have sought to justify by
various means: by appealing to Divine law as revealed, for
example, by God in the Ten Commandments; to natural law as
revealed by reason, or to the existence of an innate moral sense
revealed by intuition.

The utilitarian, on the other hand, adopts a relativist view of
ethics, and maintains that actions can be judged *only* by their
consequences and are based on the single principle of utility.
Utilitarianism seeks the greatest good of the greatest number, or,
put another way, an action is valued in direct proportion to the
benefits it produces for the highest aggregate of people. Pleasure,
happiness, aesthetic appreciation have all been put forward as the
intrinsic value for the principle of utility, but these days the

modern utilitarian is more likely to define this principle in pluralist terms by talking of social benefit. Not surprisingly, the effort to balance competing values in order to maximise benefits and minimise harms for the greatest number of people affected by a particular action can cause problems. However, this kind of consequentialist ethics is much favoured by doctors who argue with considerable fervour that most of the ethical dilemmas they face are too complex to be judged by absolute standards.

But there is another important strand in ethical thinking which is especially relevant to the doctrine of informed consent. Loosely this can be described as 'the rights of man' ethic, originated by eighteenth-century philosophers like Locke, Hume and Rousseau who, in their different ways, were proposing a theory of social contract between government and the governed based on consent, implicit rather than formal. These views later became incorporated in various Bills of Rights, most notably the American Declaration of Independence and the French Declaration of the Rights of Man. Today we prefer to call these rights 'human rights' and their scope has widened considerably, but their fundamental wellspring remains the same – a conviction that by virtue of our humanity we all possess an equal and undisputed claim to certain basic rights like life, liberty (which embraces the freedom to make our own choices) and the free expression of ideas.

Rights language has long been part of our political terminology, and from this standpoint it has been incorporated into other aspects of our social organisation such as work (the right to work, the right to form trade unions); family (guardianship rights, divorce rights); personal rights (like privacy), and, most recently, the right not to suffer discrimination on grounds of race, religion or sex.

HEALTH RIGHTS

Health care and the rights of patients are the latest entrants into the rights arena and are currently the subject of lively controversy. When and how to define clinical death, euthanasia (does the patient have a right to choose to die?), the merits of organ transplantation, abortion (the rights of the foetus versus a woman's right to choose), test-tube babies (*in vitro* fertilisation), research on embryos and other developments in genetic engineering – these are all burning topics which have created a thriving new industry for moral philosophers, scientists and lawyers. Called biomedical ethics, they are generating a profuse literature and, in some quarters, notably among many members of the medical profession, considerable alarm as the latter see their former undisputed authority threatened.

'I don't see a problem. What do you mean by moral?' is the way Mr Patrick Steptoe, pioneer doctor in the production of test-tube babies, responded in 1984 to a television interviewer who was asking him about his latest success in making women pregnant by implanting frozen embryos. The problem the rest of us see lies, of course, in the disposal of those embryos which are 'surplus to requirements'.

At a more personal level with which we can all readily identify, there is the question of patient confidentiality. When a patient gives a doctor information about herself, she sees him writing it down but she does not see what he is writing, nor does she know to whom that information may be passed on. She presumes that her notes will be seen, at most, only by those directly responsible for her treatment, but in fact this may not be so. They may be scrutinised by many pairs of eyes, not all of them even medical. Psychology students, social scientists, clerks, orderlies, voluntary workers, the hospital chaplain – the list of those who can claim for one reason or another to have a legitimate 'professional' need to gain access to this information is endless. Not only is the patient the one person who is never allowed to read her own notes but she is also never asked to give her consent to this widespread dissemination of intimate details about herself. If anyone does make a decision on her behalf it will be the doctor in charge of her case, but more often than we would like to imagine, even that safeguard is bypassed.

Another issue of vital ethical concern is resource allocation. Who is to decide which patients are to receive certain expensive treatments and on what criteria? When cuts are made in the health services, how are they justified and where should the axe fall? Why, for instance, does acute medicine receive such a large share of the capital cake when the growing needs of an ageing population and of mentally handicapped children, who would not be alive were it not for the advances in medical technology, are given such short shrift? Can it be right that thirty years after the introduction of the National Health Service we see the gap between the healthy, well-fed rich and the sick, malnourished poor actually widening, with those most in need of an efficient health service least likely to receive the benefits?*

Underpinning all these considerations is the concept of informed consent, because if we believe that the patient has a right to know about her individual circumstances in order to make the appropriate decisions, then by extension we all have a right to know about the way our health services are organised and to participate in the decisions which are made. Obviously we cannot all be in there on a day-to-day basis but we should be using our community health councils and every other means of delegated representation to make sure that our views on the broad areas of policy making are heard and considered.

To paraphrase Clemenceau, who said that 'war is too important to leave to the generals', there is a growing consensus of public opinion that medicine, and in particular medical ethics, is too important to leave to the doctors. If praise, or blame, depending on your standpoint, is to be attributed for this major shift in society's attitude towards doctors, then there are two post-war movements which can justifiably claim to share out the honours between them. One is the consumerist movement which has steadily extended the scope of its operation to include all forms of goods and services, including health care. The other – in my view much the more influential because it has encouraged the consumerists to follow in its wake – is the new wave of the women's movement which can be dated from the late sixties.

Right from the start women perceived that the way medical services were being offered to them, the content of those services and the presumptions on which they were based directly affected their rights of choice and, therefore, their right to be treated as autonomous individuals. The demand to change the abortion laws was grounded in the claim that it is 'a woman's right to choose'. A flood of literature challenging the 'myth of the medical mystique', medical paternalism (which women realised was doubly compounded for them because of their sex) and male chauvinist perceptions of women's sexuality has poured out of the movement, both here and abroad. Organisations have been formed to deal with specific issues like childbirth, the delivery of contraceptive services, cervical screening and the demand of mothers to stay with their children in hospital. Pressure has been put on doctors to review and reform their attitudes to so-called 'women's problems' such as premenstrual tension, post-natal depression,

* *The Black Report* – see Select bibliography

menopause and hysterectomy. The struggle continues, and often women feel as if they make advances only to find themselves again under siege, as when, for example, new fears are raised about dangerous side effects from the Pill or the dehumanising effects of the new technology on the experience of childbirth.

On the credit side, women are slowly acquiring confidence in their encounters with the medical profession; they are more knowledgeable about their bodies and bodily functions; they are less willing to accept prescriptions and treatments without question. And this growing assertiveness is reflected in the patient population generally. Here the media in its more responsible manifestations can also claim some credit. The thirst for medical information and facts is apparently unquenchable, and most newspapers and magazines now carry regular medical articles to meet the demand. Doctors themselves are becoming less reticent about making public statements and appearing on television. Health education has become a 'good thing', worthy of government spending, instead of being viewed as the eccentric preserve of a few doctors who were thought by their colleagues to be overly concerned with preventive rather than curative medicine. Even the growing move towards self-help and self-care which is evident in the numerous voluntary associations for people with a particular health disorder – kidney failure, cancer, multiple sclerosis, stroke, depression and many more – is now welcomed by doctors rather than disapproved of as formerly, although we have to beware of mistaking genuine conviction for a sentiment of *laissez-faire* engendered by the health cuts.

What have all these changes of attitude towards health care got to do with informed consent? In my view everything, because they are also symptomatic of raised expectations, of ourselves as much as of our doctors. We are no longer prepared to be humble and submissive in the presence of authority, however benevolently disposed. We know more and we therefore expect to be treated as equals, even if the doctor does have the advantage of professional skills and experience. We also expect more of our doctors – sometimes quite unreasonably – which makes us more critical of their performance. Knowledge, like love, grows upon the appetite it feeds. The more we know, the more we feel it is our right always to be informed and consulted. The right to choose between options, the right to make our own decisions, in short the right to be asked for our informed consent, whether in the context of clinical practice or clinical trials, is the natural expression of our increased sense of autonomy in matters medical.

Before considering how we justify this right to know, we need to understand more precisely what we mean by rights: on what they are based; the implications they have for our own actions, and the obligations they impose on others.

MORAL AND LEGAL RIGHTS

Rights are defined in terms of claims and they are based on an acknowledged principle which may be moral or may be legal. To prove a moral right exists you have to prove that it is grounded in certain principles which apply universally. If you possess that moral right, so does everyone else. However, a moral right is not necessarily legally enforceable, although if enough people feel sufficiently outraged by the flagrant abuse of a recognised moral right they may demand legislation to protect that right. This is the way many laws come into being, particularly those to do with rights based on the principle of autonomy, like the right to practise homosexuality (positive) or the right not to suffer discrimination on grounds of sex (negative).

A legal right, on the other hand, does not have to be supported by any moral principle. *Per se* it is not concerned with good or bad, only with what is right or what is wrong according to the definition of the law enforcing it. Laws can be bad and laws can be changed, whereas the essence of a moral right is that it is based on a moral principle which is seen to be intrinsically good and, therefore, not subject to change. The problem arises when we have to consider the claims of what appear to be conflicting moral rights based on different moral principles. Although monist philosophers of a Kantian frame of mind would argue that there is only one supreme moral principle from which all others derive their authority, most people are pragmatic pluralists who do not see life as either clear cut or single track. We spend our time performing a balancing act, weighing alternatives and making decisions in relation to other people's rights as well as our own, in the full realisation that we cannot enjoy exclusive personal autonomy.

The rights of patients in health care are narrowly defined. Legally a doctor can be sued for battery (unlawful touching) and for negligence (the failure to meet approved professional standards of care). Patient consent is a key issue in cases of battery, but agreeing to a procedure is not the same as giving your informed consent. Many patients agree to procedures without understanding what they are about or why they are being asked to agree. These distinctions between forms of consent will be considered more closely in chapter 3. Meanwhile, since informed consent is not a legal right in this country we must examine the moral grounds on which we base our claim to this right and determine whether it can be justified.

FEELINGS ARE NOT ENOUGH

The doctrine of informed consent in medical practice arouses strong feelings on all sides. Those who believe that it is a right which cannot be questioned and who base their claim uniquely on the individual's right to self-determination – the principle of autonomy – sometimes refuse to give credence to the very real dilemmas facing doctors in their everyday practice. Many doctors, on the other hand, who base their philosophy of action on their Hippocratic oath (see Appendix A) to act in the best interests of their patients, will argue that the obligation to seek informed consent is often not necessary, sometimes undesirable and frequently impossible. In short, they do not accept that they have this obligation. They will recount from experience many examples of patients explicitly requesting not to know – 'It's up to you doctor, you know best' – and of patients making it clear from the form of their questions that what they are seeking is not the truth but reassurance. The patient who asks, 'I haven't got cancer, have I?' may really be saying 'Don't tell me if I have.' Others will argue that the whole idea of informed consent is a myth. A lay person, so the argument goes, cannot possibly understand the medical implications of her or his condition nor the technical details of the treatment proposed. Knowledge which doctors have acquired through years of training and clinical practice cannot possibly be imparted to someone, however intelligent or well-educated, who does not share the same scientific background. Pushed to its logical conclusion, this argument invariably ends with the statement: 'Look, doctors themselves don't know *everything* about a particular condition, so there's no way they can ever "fully" inform the patient.'

I believe we should respect these arguments even while refuting them. We must remember that doctors are at the sharp end of the line. We consult them because we need medical attention and they have the expertise, but sometimes we entertain wholly unreasonable expectations of their omniscience and omnipotence. We expect them to come up with answers which they may not be able to give us and to provide cures which they may not be able to achieve. Doctors, for their part, have been guilty of pandering to these false hopes because it makes their job easier if patients accept their authority without question. Their claim that it is their duty to make decisions on behalf of their patients without involving them more than superficially in the decision-making process has gone unchallenged until recently.

Today, as we know, there is a growing lay opinion, shared by many doctors, that they should present choices to their patients and seek their consent. But if that obligation is to be taken seriously, then we must also accept that in claiming our right to be informed we too will have to shoulder new responsibilities, because rights entail obligations, both on those who claim them and on those from whom they are claimed. And moral rights, to be valid, must be based on principles which are generally accepted as moral.

THE FIVE PRINCIPLES

The principle of *autonomy* has already been mentioned several times in passing, and for good reason, because it is the key principle which validates the doctrine of informed consent. Autonomy can be defined as the individual's freedom to decide her or his goals and to act according to those goals. Inherent in this principle is the notion of personal responsibility. Because we believe human beings to be rational we regard them as persons rather than objects or things. A person is a self-determining individual who is able to think about ends, and decide on the means by which she or he intends to fulfil those ends. This same thinking, self-determining person is also a social human being, so the likelihood of her or his being able to take any action in isolation, without either being influenced by social factors or affecting someone somehow, is remote. However, if we take the Kantian line that persons are ends in themselves and should not be used as means by other persons (and it would be difficult to gainsay this view), then we must believe that the principle of autonomy, even if it cannot be the overriding principle on all occasions, is nonetheless extremely important.

Whatever our social philosophy, we all recognise that there are important occasions in our lives when we put ourselves first, that we have a right to do this, and that this right is generally accepted. Illness is one of those times. The body we inhabit is ours and ours alone to decide about, which does not mean that in coming to our decisions we do not consider, and more often than not take, the advice given to us by doctors. We also consider the effects our decisions may have on other people, especially those in a close relation to us. But when all the chips are down we think first and last of ourselves alone. In such circumstances we think of ourselves as being our own ends and we expect others to respect that view of ourselves – just as they expect us to respect them in the same way.

To think of persons as ends in themselves gives them an intrinsic value which demands respect, even if we do not always approve of their actions or the judgements on which they are based. The principle of autonomy does not of itself confer either respectability or morality on the autonomous action and, indeed, many such actions can be highly reprehensible. Nor would any but the most rigid autonomist maintain that human beings must always and at all times act autonomously without any consideration of other people's equal claim to autonomy. Providing we *freely* concede our autonomy to a legitimate authority for specific purposes, as we do in a democratic system, then our fundamental autonomy is preserved.

The notion of what constitutes a legitimate authority is, of course, crucial and should be constantly under review in an alert society. Only lately has this concern been extended to the field of medical ethics. Doctors have always emphasised the importance of authority in their relationship with their patients and based their own claim to clinical autonomy, the right to make decisions on the patient's behalf, on that authority. But do they have a right to assume that patients, in surrendering their bodies to doctors for medical care, have also surrendered their right to self-determination? Surely not, if we accept that the principle of autonomy is a valid moral principle and therefore constant and unable to be 'altered as it alteration finds'. And if we further accept that it is defined in terms of the individual's right to make independent decisions relating to privately determined goals, then we must accept that it applies to all persons in all circumstances unless they consciously resign that right or, for some reason, are unable to exercise it. (Exceptions are discussed in chapter 3.)

Deeply embedded in the principle of autonomy is the concept of 'respect for persons', and one of the ways of expressing that respect is always to assume that they wish to exercise their rights unless they indicate otherwise. In the medical context, that respect between persons for persons is expressed by doctors *enabling* patients to give their informed consent. That, in practical terms, means offering them the opportunity to be informed as much or as little as they require. To do less than that is to deny them their autonomy. But it is equally a denial of autonomy to force unwanted information on those who have clearly indicated, not necessarily verbally, that they do not want it. Respect for persons and for their autonomy implies that we also respect their right *not* to exercise their autonomy in given circumstances or, alternatively, their right to make choices which we may consider to be unwise or irresponsible.

The principle of *veracity* (truthfulness) is, as Sissela Bok discovered when she came to write her penetrating enquiry *Lying, Moral Choice in Public and Private Life*, hardly given a mention in the medical ethical literature. Yet trust, which can only be based on accepting this principle, is an obsessive concern with doctors in their relationship with their patients. Doctors expect their patients to trust them to act always in their best interests, to prescribe only treatments which they consider to be beneficial and to place their skills and their experience at the disposal of their patients. Doctors value their patients' trust, not least because they know that without it their job would be virtually impossible. Sometimes they trade on it. 'My patients do as they are told because they trust me' is often boasted by doctors who, in the following breath, will explain why 'white' lies are sometimes necessary and informed consent is virtually impossible.

'Telling the truth can be dangerously misleading and cause a great deal of unhappiness,' one doctor was at pains to explain to me. He cited his experience of telling the mother of an eleven-year-old boy that the child ran a one to two per cent risk of blindness if he was given radiotherapy to get rid of a non-malignant tumour; on the other hand, if it was left untreated it would spread and he would certainly go blind. The child survived the radiotherapy unscathed but the mother ('foolish woman' was the unspoken comment) was tortured by the belief that the child could go blind at any time. Maybe this woman was unduly over-anxious, but it could just be that by now she has been reassured by seeing her son in continuing good health. Our emotions are, in a crisis, usually more powerful influences on our judgement than our reason, as even those who most pride themselves on keeping their cool are obliged to admit, if they are honest. Just how would this same doctor have felt if he had not been frank with her and, by an evil chance, the boy's cure had blinded him? The mother could have accused him, with perfect justification but alas little satisfaction, that he had concealed a vital risk factor from her.

Doctors do not like to confess to their own doubts and worries; indeed they regard such revelations as a sign of weakness, a threat to the patient's morale and a major offence against the canon of trust in the patient-doctor relationship. But who has established this canon of trust? And why is it that trust is almost uniquely discussed in terms of the patient's confidence in the doctor? Seldom do we hear about doctors trusting their patients by, for example, allowing them to see their medical records. Worse still, as we have already noted, the patient's confidence that the information she discloses will be treated as confidential is frequently abused.

Trust between two people, if it is to mean anything, must be reciprocal. They trust each other to observe the same rules of discretion and to respect each other equally as persons, regardless of the differences in their social or material circumstances which may, indeed, be hugely unequal.

A trust is broken when one party to the relationship deceives the other in some way, irrespective of whether the deceived party discovers the deception. But, of course, if we do catch out the trusted person in a lie, then our sense of outrage is acute. We feel we have been duped, manipulated and coerced; we have been deprived of information; we have possibly made choices which we would not have made had we been fully aware of the facts, or, worse still, we have been deprived of choice altogether. In a medical situation none of these feelings does the patient any good, yet such circumstances often arise and, too often, they are blandly ignored by doctors.

In asking their patients to trust them it would seem only fair that doctors should reward that trust by dealing honestly with them. Seeking the informed consent of their patients is part of that honest relationship. Yet there are some doctors who will argue with total sincerity that the only way to preserve that trust is to withhold information or even tell a downright lie. Their justifications for this paradoxical view are examined more fully in chapter 8. Here we will observe only that the principle of veracity which is widely accepted, even if not always practised, as a moral principle appears to be dispensable in certain medical situations. What we will ultimately question is whether those special circumstances are ever sufficient in themselves to permit doctors the liberty to go against normally accepted standards of trust, especially when we know that often the deception is about a matter of intense concern to the person who is being deceived. This professionally approved licence to lie makes the phrase 'a relationship of mutual trust and respect' so frequently used by doctors to describe their relationship with their patients sound hollow indeed.

The principles of autonomy and veracity are the two most important principles in favour of informed consent. Autonomy is the condition of our claim to be responsible for our own destinies. Veracity, which is the cornerstone of our relationship with others, honours that claim. Next in importance comes the principle of *justice* which acknowledges the claim for patient autonomy by enabling it to be exercised. (The principle of justice also has many other important applications in health care: for example, in resource allocation.)

However we choose to describe the patient-doctor relationship – as a contract, a covenant, or a partnership – it implies that both parties have a duty to treat each other justly. Ideally, doctors should respect the confidence and trust of their patients and seek to meet their personal needs while at the same time balancing the rights of all their other patients to similar attention and care. Ideally, patients should respect the judgement and skills of their doctors and seek to help them by co-operating with treatment procedures and by not making undue demands on them that would prejudice the right of other patients to receive the same attention. If both sides are to meet as equals, as 'joint adventurers in a common cause' as Paul Ramsey, the ethicist, defines the relationship in his book *The Patient as Person*, then the principle of justice requires this equal though different contribution from each of the parties. Implicit in this joint undertaking of equals is the principle of informed consent. If the doctor does not confide in the patient as the patient confides in the doctor, then the relationship is unequal and unjust. To quote Ramsey again, 'Consent expresses or establishes this relationship, and the requirement of consent sustains it.'

Additionally, there are two other principles to consider, especially as they are sometimes invoked by doctors as reasons for *not* seeking informed consent.

The principle of *beneficence* implies the duty to do good. In the negative sense this is interpreted as preventing harm; in the positive sense it means producing benefits of some kind. Doctors understand beneficence as their duty to act in the best interests of their patients, a duty which is hallowed by the Hippocratic tradition and which they have always considered to be their guiding principle of action. I doubt that anyone would wish doctors not to believe in this principle; our trust in them is nourished by knowing that they act according to this belief. But there are some problems about its practice.

Quite simply, who is to decide what are the best interests of the patient? Doctors generally have no hesitation in saying that they must, because their skills and experience give them the advantage of superior knowledge. They understand better than any non-medically qualified person the aetiology (causes) and likely course of the disease they are treating; they appreciate the medical consequences of the decisions they make. And when they do have doubts in a particular case they can draw on the resources of their colleagues. Their patients have put themselves into their hands precisely because they possess these skills and they rely on their doctors to choose the best treatment for them.

Well and good if that is all that constitutes the 'best interests' of a patient. But does it? In real life we well know that there are occasions when something which seems best to one person can be quite the opposite for another. For instance, how often do we read in a newspaper account that someone who has been thrown into deep shock by some traumatic incident, say the loss of her children in a fire, has been put under heavy sedation? To the doctors this may seem like the only proper, compassionate course of action, and maybe for some people it is; for others, however, dulling the agony now may only drive the grief inwards so deeply that the bereaved person never fully recovers.

A woman who lost her husband in a swimming accident had her memory wiped out by three weeks of solid sedation. Because she had not been allowed to live through her desperation at the time, she spent years in a coma of depression, finally expunging the savage guilt she felt only by going on a wild shoplifting spree which ended up in the locked ward of a mental hospital. At last, she was able to unburden herself and find release from the mental torture she had been suffering by being allowed to relive those dreadful last moments when she had pushed off the drowning man clutching at her in order to save herself.

Obviously, we cannot expect doctors to have divine insight about everything relating to their patients' lives, but a story like this illustrates the need for caution in assuming that one solution will suit all and sundry. Real life does not stop in the doctor's waiting room or at the hospital gates. People carry with them in sickness as in health all their personal luggage of hopes, fears, beliefs, experiences, prejudices, expectations and the particular circumstances of their individual existence; becoming a patient does not turn them into a non-person, a 'case' for treatment.

Of course doctors must tell their patients what they think is in their best interests – it would be highly unethical if they did not – but this should not prevent them from seeking also to see things from their patients' perspective. Someone who has already been through a great deal of pain and distress as a result of her disease may reject the idea of further treatment, even though it holds out the hope of living a little longer. What doctors call heroic surgery and we would call dire mutilation, or yet another drastically toxic regime of chemotherapy to hold off encroaching cancer, may simply make that last scrap of life unbearable for the patient. In such circumstances it would be wrong for the doctor to pull rank either by insisting that the treatment was necessary or persuading the patient to accept it by minimising the side effects, especially when we consider how many of these 'wonder treatments' are subsequently discarded.

Fifteen years ago, for example, a woman suffering from breast cancer had been through most of the treatments then available. She knew she was dying and had made all her preparations, but she was persuaded to submit to one more operation – removal of the pituitary gland. This left her face so badly bruised that she put off seeing her children for several days to spare them the shock of her appearance. She saw them only once more before she died. The operation is now recognised to be useless for this particular condition.

If beneficence is left entirely to the subjective judgement of doctors it too easily becomes an excuse for paternalism. But if patients are allowed to exercise their equal right to make subjective judgements on their own behalf and to state what they consider to be their own 'best interests', then it can act as a useful measure for assessing the pros and cons of a particular decision. When doctors apply *only* the principle of beneficence to medical research, and to clinical trials in particular, the interests of the individual patient tend to lose out against the interests of future generations of patients. However, if beneficence is considered *together* with the principle of autonomy then it would seem only proper that the decision as to whether to enter a clinical trial must rest with the patient, not the doctor. As a self-determining person it is in the patient's 'best interest' to make that decision, but of course this is possible only if the doctor enables the patient to give informed consent.

The principle of *nonmaleficence* is the reverse aspect of beneficence. *Primum non nocere* (also attributed to Hippocrates) is a positive principle not to do harm as opposed to merely preventing harm. The distinction is subtle but real and it applies particularly to the doctor's duty to act with due care and avoid negligence. It also assumes a special significance in the context of clinical trials where submitting a new treatment to study under controlled conditions can be justified only if it is believed that it will not produce risks or harms greater than the standard therapy with which it is being compared. The aim of the study is, of course, to discover which treatment produces the most benefits. (The structure and ethical implications of clinical trials are fully discussed in Part Two.)

Beneficence and maleficence are often balanced against each other to determine conflicting priorities in medical care: how scarce resources should be allocated and which groups of patients have a prior claim to certain services. For example, is the harm some women will suffer because they are not in the decreed age group for breast cancer screening going to be greater than the benefits which will be produced by restricting the service to an identifiable high-risk population? The problem about balancing these claims is the familiar utilitarian difficulty of how exactly you measure the distribution of these aggregated benefits and harms.

When so much is a matter of guesswork, the field is wide open for interested parties in the medical world to fight for their competing claims and forget the most interested party of all – the patient, who is in danger of being cut out as the cuts start biting. We see this happening all the time: a doctor announces that his funds have been slashed so he will no longer be able to carry on his valuable but extremely specialised work for a small group of patients. If the appeal is sufficiently heart-rending – anything to do with children or cancer patients arouses an immediate response, which is guaranteed to be whipped up by media publicity – the doctor is overwhelmed by donations, and the DHSS announces that it has changed its mind and promises to support the work. This probably means that the money allocated for some other equally important but infinitely less glamorous area of health care, like developing aids for the physically handicapped or improving geriatric services, is eaten into, yet again. What is questionable in this kind of situation is not the nature of the work – nobody would want to deny a child its chance to live – but that too often we allow our priorities in health care to be determined by emotional appeal rather than by a cooler appraisal of the total needs of the population.

We, the public, need to be educated together with doctors, researchers *and* the government officials responsible for policy-making in how to make a more just distribution of the resources available. I repeat the point I made earlier in this chapter. Exercising our right to informed consent is important not just for us as individuals but for us as members of a society which professes concern for everyone living in our community. That is why I maintain that although the patient's right to informed consent is by no means the only right in health care it could be the supreme right. To discover whether there are any valid grounds for this assumption we must now examine what *we*, the potential patients, mean by informed consent, its purpose for *us* in the patient-doctor relationship, and how and when we expect to exercise our right to give it, or refuse it.

3 Understanding consent – the right to say no

> What is above all needed is to let the meaning choose
> the word, and not the other way round ... the worst
> thing one can do with words is to surrender to them.
>
> George Orwell, *Politics and the English Language*

'Informed consent' is in danger of becoming a totem slogan,
confined to the exclusive circles of medicine and law, where it is
freely brandished as much by those who would deny it meaning
of any kind as by those who claim that it says everything. What we
have to do now is wrest it from the grasp of the professionals and
decide, with a little bit of help from the philosophers and the
grammarians, whether it truly expresses our understanding of
consent. This is not obtuse pedantry. An important principle lies
behind a deceptively simple formula; its words are burdened with
shades of meaning which we must clarify in our own minds before
we can know how to use it.

SORTING OUT THE SEMANTICS

Consent comes from the Latin *consentire*, which means to feel or
think together. The original simple meaning of agreeing or 'being
in accord' has been expanded: in current usage consent is defined
as a *voluntary* compliance, or as a permission. 'I consent' means 'I
freely agree to your proposal', which is an explicit statement that
my consent to a certain course of action has been sought and
granted without any element of coercion. Implicitly this definition
includes the notion of choice and, therefore, the possibility of
refusal.

By adding on 'informed' to 'consent', the concept immediately acquires a significantly different dimension. An informed person is someone who is instructed, who knows the facts. We also use 'informed' in a more particular sense to denote someone who is educated, intelligent and more knowledgeable than most about a special subject. Whereas an informed person in the first sense may know the facts without necessarily understanding their causes or requiring detailed explanations, the second kind of informed person is quite likely to consider herself *un*informed unless she understands as much as possible. This distinction becomes crucial when we consider some of the questions which the concept of 'informed consent' raises in a medical context. For example, is the consent given by a partially informed person in some way incomplete and, therefore, of diminished value compared to the consent afforded by someone who has made it her business to be fully informed? Could it be that the idea that we can ever be 'fully informed' is itself something of a nonsense – 'the myth of informed consent', as many have described it? And if it is a myth, then how can we possibly insist that informed consent is not merely a valid concept, but that it is also our right?

These questions are not as hard to answer as some would like to suggest. It is a matter of analysing the component elements of both words and then putting them together again to establish their total meaning. We have to understand their interrelationship before we can grasp the whole picture. In the process it is quite possible that 'informed consent' will turn out not to convey exactly what we first thought it to mean, in which case it may be necessary to qualify it further or even offer an alternative form of words.

As we have already noted, the elements of *choice* and *voluntariness* are essential to the concept of consent. Choice implies that we are aware of at least one alternative to the action proposed – that of saying no – but of course there may be several other positive possibilities open to us which we can know about only if we are informed of their existence. The voluntary element indicates that we give our consent freely, unhampered by any hint of coercion such as a threat to refuse treatment if we do not accept 'doctor's orders'. A more subtle form of coercion is to withhold certain information which the person seeking the consent has good reason to believe might influence the other person not to give it. For example, if a doctor proposes an operation to a patient but omits to tell her that it is an operation of choice and is not the only possible treatment for her condition, then the doctor is practising coercion by deceit. The patient has been deluded into thinking that her options are more restricted than they really are and so she gives her consent under false pretences. This is not consent as we normally understand it, yet many doctors do exactly this when they argue that the patient's consent can be implied by the very act of seeking their advice and that no further explicit statement of agreement is required.

Choice and voluntariness are both conditional on the understanding that the relevant information is made available. *Competence*, the third element in consent, also depends indirectly on information in that the person whose consent is sought must understand that that is what is being asked and, to some extent, the reasons for seeking it, although her comprehension does not have to be profound. Competence is not a standard of general ability; it is merely a measure we use to determine whether a person is adequately equipped to perform a specific task. A patient who is seriously ill with cancer may be incompetent to understand the technical details of the treatment proposed – for instance, she will not know about the specific qualities of the drugs or why they are used in a certain combination – but this ignorance does not make her incompetent to decide whether she wishes to consent to it. The test of her competence to give consent is measured by two rules: she must know that she is giving it and she must understand what it involves. By this measure most people are competent to give, or refuse, their consent, but they do need to be adequately informed about the possible consequences of their decision.

Disclosure and *understanding* are, therefore, the two crucial elements in any valid transaction of information. The responsibility for disclosing an adequate amount of information and endeavouring to ensure that it has been understood lies with the informant, the person who is seeking the consent. What we have to determine now is whether these conditions are realistic and attainable in the medical context.

The relationship between patient and doctor is not a legal contract but it is fiduciary, in other words it is based on an implicit relationship of trust. Moreover, the circumstances in which it exists are usually of extreme importance to the patient. How is it, then, that doctors claim a unique right to exempt themselves on occasion from obligations which others who are in a similar relationship – priests, lawyers and bank managers for example – recognise and attempt to meet? In ordinary clinical practice patients are often told much less than they would like to know about their condition unless they press hard and know the right questions to ask. And in clinical trials, a request from those doctors running the trial that informed consent should *not* be sought is too often sanctioned by ethical committees. Yet most patients are no less competent than healthy people to understand the terms of their consent. We shall be examining in detail these special circumstances which doctors feel entitle them to claim 'therapeutic privilege' later in this chapter (*Exceptions*) and in Part Two. Meanwhile we have to establish how much information a reasonable person has a right to expect from her doctor.

THE REASONABLE PERSON

Experience teaches us that it can be very difficult to decide exactly how much information should be disclosed to meet the criteria of a truly informed consent. In particular, how does either party to the dialogue know that an adequate degree of information has been provided? Communicating specialised knowledge to someone who is untutored in the subject is a problem in any field. Expertise generates its own jargon, and nowhere more so than in medicine. Doctors have the advantage of their skills and the clinical experience which they bring to their decision-making. Patients on the other hand are usually ignorant about the basic medical facts relating to their illness and they are further handicapped by their vulnerable emotional state. A seriously ill person is certain to be deeply worried and fearful, and is usually in no condition to absorb difficult technical information.

The ugly class divisions in our society also have to be taken into account. Doctors are invariably middle class, by virtue of their education if not their origins, whereas a large number of their patients will be working class. This puts the latter at a distinct disadvantage when it comes to voicing their preferences or doubts to someone who speaks with a different accent, almost in a different language and who is surrounded by the trappings of authority. Doctors (much more than nurses) often find it very difficult to avoid talking down to their patients when trying to explain complex facts and the patients are inhibited in their responses because they feel they cannot express

36   *Whose body is it?*

themselves 'properly', even when they know perfectly well that there
are questions they would like to ask. Worried that they may be wasting
the doctor's time, intimidated by the hospital aura, and often
conditioned to believe that doctor knows best, they may be quite
genuinely frightened of saying anything which might upset the
doctor.

The dilemma this causes for both patient and doctor is acute and
should not be underestimated, but these obstacles to communication
must be overcome. Somehow we have to find an objective standard of
measurement if we believe that the patient, whoever she is, has as
equal a right as any other person to give her informed consent to
important decisions affecting her welfare. In view of the life and death
nature of some of these decisions, it can be argued that the patient's
right to informed consent requires special safeguards (see chapter 9).

As we saw in the previous chapter, doctors who use the principle of
beneficence as their guideline for action are led all too easily into
making paternalistic assessments of their patient's best interests. Some
outrightly reject the doctrine of informed consent, seeing it as no more
than mischievous cant promulgated by lawyers, moralists and other
would-be-goods who are poking their noses into an area of human
affairs about which they know next to nothing. And then there are
those who, suffering from an overdose of literal-mindedness, adopt
the *reductio ad absurdum* style of reasoning.

F.J. Ingelfinger has produced a sophisticated variation of this
argument in his much-quoted paper, 'Informed (but uneducated)
consent', in which he states that the patients' understanding of their
medical situation will always be markedly inferior to the understanding of 'the responsible medical investigator [who] understands
the goals, nature and hazards of his study'.* He presents persuasive
evidence to show that doctors can give patients any number of facts
without succeeding in enabling them to achieve any real understanding of their significance. But what is significant for whom?

Ingelfinger's type of argument is dangerously fallacious in that it
assumes that understanding the mechanism and purposes of the study
(or treatment) is the only understanding in question. It is true that the
patient may very well not understand the intricacies or the long-term
objectives of a particular course of action as it has been conceived by

* *New England Journal of Medicine*, 1972, 287: 465-66

the researcher-doctor, but this does not prevent her understanding perfectly adequately its direct significance for her, providing, of course, that it has been properly explained to her. The Ingelfinger view of what it means to be informed is idiosyncratic if not perverse. It is certainly not one which normally pertains in similar non-medical circumstances where consent to a particular action is being sought. For example, the lawyer who advises a client about the pros and cons of pursuing a property claim is not expected to 'educate' her client by reading out all the legal references and precedents on which she bases her opinion, unless the client happens to be of a particularly enquiring mind. The average client requires only two things to enable her to make a decision: first, the 'material evidence', that is sufficient and specific information directly related to the type of action being contemplated; and second, that this information should be conveyed to her in non-technical language which enables her to understand its relevance to her particular situation.

The doctor's patient requires no more but certainly no less than the lawyer's client. This brings us back to the essential conditions for obtaining a 'valid informed consent': there must be *adequate* disclosure from the informant met by adequate understanding from the person receiving the information, thus enabling the latter freely to give or refuse her consent.

The 'reasonable person' is you, me and every other adult, autonomous human being who normally expects to make decisions according to our own perceptions of what is reasonable for us. Reasonable people have reason in common, but the reasons we may have for adopting a particular course of action can be hugely variable. The fact that one person disagrees with another's reasons, regarding them as foolish or even irrational, is not a valid reason for preventing someone from determining her own actions, unless of course the person is patently unreasonable because of mental derangement and liable to harm herself or others. Evidently, reasonableness is not the exclusive prerogative of the doctor or a body of medical experts, nor are their good intentions usually in doubt, but their desire to seek consent inevitably opens the door to the possibility that they might be tempted to present the information in a biased or partial way. Therefore, the objective standards by which a reasonable person (the patient) would expect to give consent must be judged by those from whom the consent is sought and not left to the judgement of those who seek it (the doctors).

In an ordinary clinical situation, when, for example, the patient has just been told that she should have a hysterectomy, she will want to know why the doctor thinks this is necessary, whether he thinks her condition is malignant or whether it is due to fibroids or some similar condition causing her excessive pain and discomfort. She may not know that there are different kinds of hysterectomy, so the doctor should volunteer this information and tell her exactly what her operation will involve and what kind of after-effects to expect. An enquiring patient might demand much more information and run the risk of being branded as tiresome and 'unreasonable' for her pains. And she may well not get all the answers she seeks because doctors are not legally obliged to tell their patients any more than *they* think it is necessary to disclose (see chapter 4).

There are, of course, patients who really want to know as little as possible about their illness; especially, they do not want to be told it is really serious. Here a doctor has to tread very carefully. Some information he must volunteer, but if he sees that the patient is shutting herself off from hearing too much although agreeing to his proposals for treatment, then he is justified in presuming that she is giving her consent. Unfortunately, this kind of signalling from the patient is usually expressed tacitly and the doctor has to be alert to the possibility that she might well change her mind later. The duty to keep the dialogue open remains always with the doctor.

If a doctor wishes to enter his patient into a clinical trial the 'reasonable person' could reasonably expect even more stringent objective standards from him for seeking her informed consent. Say it is a trial testing two different treatments for a serious heart condition. One involves surgery, the other a course of drugs. The doctor should explain the purpose of the trial and why the patient has been selected for it (which could mean revealing an unfavourable prognosis). He must explain how the trial is structured and if this means that the patient will be randomly allocated to one or other of the treatments he must be prepared to explain the scientific reasons for this procedure. As we shall see in Part Two, this is not done easily, but it is necessary because the patient will quite reasonably want to know why the doctor has not got a firm opinion about the best treatment for her. He must explain all the known risks and benefits accruing to both treatments and warn her that there may be unknown side effects. Finally, and most important, he must make it clear to her that she is at liberty to withdraw her consent *at any time* during the progress of the trial, a liberty which he too has, should he think at some stage that the treatment she has been allocated is not proving beneficial. All in all, the doctor has to be as thoroughly convinced that the patient really understands what she is committing herself to as the patient herself.

Interestingly, these conditions for obtaining a patient's informed consent to participating in a clinical trial have not been dreamed up by pedantic ethicists to conform with the 'reasonable person's' standards; they have been defined as necessary by doctors themselves (see chapter 4). The reasons doctors offer for not always obeying their own code are the central theme of this book.

It is, however, for the patient to decide – with the doctor's co-operation – how much information is necessary. Some patients will want to know a lot, others will be content with the bare outlines, and some will prefer to know nothing. To force undesired information on the latter is as much a violation of their autonomy as it is the denial of information to those who want it.

EXCEPTIONS

There are, of course, categories of patients who cannot be described as 'reasonable persons' because they are not competent to give consent. Children, the severely retarded, the elderly senile and people in a coma are all incompetent to give a valid consent, but for different reasons. Consent for their treatment has to be sought from a second party – a parent, relative or legal guardian.

Only the profoundly mentally handicapped person can be deemed to be totally and permanently incompetent. The unconscious patient who is the victim of an accident or a stroke suffers from *temporary* incompetence, and if there is no one available to give consent on her behalf, the doctor giving her life-saving treatment is justified in assuming what Paul Ramsey calls a 'constructive consent', meaning she would agree to it if she were in a state to do so. This presumption may not, of course, be true in the case of a person who has failed in a suicide attempt: for example, someone who comes round after having had her stomach pumped for a drug overdose may complain bitterly that she wishes she had been allowed to die. It seems clear, though, that no matter whether the attempt proves to have been 'a cry for help' or a genuine intention to end her life, the doctor's conscience combined with the medical duty to save life must overrule what can only be a guess at the patient's motivation. If it were not, we would all feel permanently insecure with our doctors.

Children and the elderly senile suffer from *limited* competence. Both groups of patients may understand in a very simple sense that their consent is required – the doctor asks the child to undress for an injection or explains to the confused old lady that she needs to take a medicine – but neither of these patients will necessarily understand the implications of her consent. Children have their parents to look after them but the elderly patient living alone constitutes a particular problem. Even regular visits from a social worker cannot ensure that she will continue to follow the doctor's instructions, yet many such patients are entered into clinical trials to test drugs, say for arthritis, without being covered by adequate supervision and follow up (see also chapter 6).

Finally, there is the perplexing category of the mentally ill. Although some of these patients may be incapable of looking after themselves or their affairs, they may be *intermittently* competent to give consent. Some of the time they may be as lucid and aware as any sane person and certainly fully capable of understanding that their consent is needed and what it implies. Determining whether they are competent to agree to a particular proposal poses a continuing problem for their doctors, particularly since so much in psychiatric treatment is still highly controversial and unresolved among doctors themselves. A mental patient who objects to a course of electro-convulsive therapy (ECT), for instance, may be no more 'irrational' than a cancer patient who refuses chemotherapy. In both cases, the patient may be quite rationally questioning whether the effects of the treatment will improve the quality of her life as she sees it.

There is a famous case in British law (*Bolam* v. *Friern Hospital Management Committee* 1957) of a patient's bringing a case of negligence against his consultant on grounds which included his failure to disclose the risk of fracture (which the patient suffered) as a result of applying ECT without anaesthetic. At the time there were two schools of thought on the procedure, some doctors believing that it was advisable to give patients a relaxant. The judge found in favour of the doctor saying that he was not negligent if he practised his professional skills according to accepted medical standards. He further added that in view of the patient's mental state at the time and the doctor's belief that ECT provided 'his only hope of cure . . . the doctor cannot be criticised if he does not stress the dangers, which he believed to be minimal . . .'

The question the court saw as the main issue in this case was the doctor's competence, not the patient's. However, Culver and Gert, who devote a good deal of attention to this subject in their illuminating book *Philosophy in Medicine*,* make the telling point that a patient's apparently irrational refusal of consent should never be taken as a sign of incompetence if, were it to have been *given* in the same circumstances, the consent would have been regarded as valid.

Drugs given to patients to modify their disordered or severely antisocial behaviour (as, for example, with sex offenders), and irreversible psychosurgery performed for the same reasons, both pose severe problems about consent. Under Section 43 of the Mental Health (Amendment) Act 1982, three people, only one of whom may be a doctor, are required to confirm that the patient both understands the nature and purpose of the treatment and has given her consent.

Proxy consent throws up further problems. Those who are asked to give consent on behalf of an incompetent patient must themselves endeavour to understand as fully as possible the nature of the consent, and they must have the patient's best interests at heart. There is no escape from paternalism in this situation but if we are obliged to choose between the doctor or the person giving the proxy consent, then it may seem obvious that the priority should lie with the latter. But turn this into a real-life situation and we see how complex and well nigh insoluble the issue can be.

Take the case of parents who have a baby which has been born desperately handicapped. One set of parents faced with this tragedy may beg the doctors to do all they can to keep the child alive, sincerely believing that some sort of life is better than none, whereas another couple will take the opposite view, pleading that the only compassionate action is to let the child die as soon as possible. The doctors caught up in this distressing dilemma may be divided among themselves, both on medical and moral grounds. Whereas one doctor will be bleakly pessimistic about the kind of life such a child would have were it allowed to live, another may think that it does have some

* See under chapter references

sort of future. One doctor will question whether the first couple fully understands the consequences of asking for the child's life to be saved; another doctor will believe that the second couple has no right to condemn the child to death. Who decides?

In the case of *Regina* v. *Leonard John Henry Arthur* 1981, it was the doctor who took the decision. A senior pediatrician at Derby City Hospital, he was called in to examine a new-born baby who had been diagnosed by the midwife as having Down's Syndrome. After talking to the parents, Dr Arthur wrote in his case notes: 'Parents do not wish baby to survive. Nursing care only.' He prescribed a narcotic analgesic, dihydrocodeine, and said that water only was to be administered. Three days later the child died. Dr Arthur's action was reported to the 'Life' organisation and he was subsequently prosecuted on a charge of murder, a charge which the judge changed to attempted murder early on in the trial when it was shown that the drug could not be proved to have caused the child's death. The doctor was subsequently acquitted by the jury, but this verdict resolves neither the limits of proxy consent nor indeed the far more fundamental problem of whether and when it is ever right to bring about the death of another human being, for whatever humane and compassionate reasons. (Helga Kuhse's paper 'A Modern Myth' (under chapter reference) offers a fascinating discussion of the ethical problems posed by this case.)

Proxy consent is equally problematic when it is required for entering an 'incompetent' patient into a clinical trial. For example, are parents entitled to consent to their child's being entered into a trial from which it will receive no direct benefit, even if there are no apparent risks in the treatment proposed? Can a son or daughter consent to their elderly senile parent's being entered into a similar type of research study when the treatment is not immediately beneficial to the patients involved but could produce results which will be useful for future generations of geriatric patients? The law is on the side of these people, saying that no one, however helpless and incapacitated, is ever the property of anyone else. Whatever the individual's mental or physical condition, she remains a member of the human race and as such has the right to be considered always as an end in herself, never as the means to someone else's ends, even though she is unable to assert that right for herself. The parent's or guardian's relationship to an incapable patient is fiduciary: they are in a position of trust and their primary duty, which they share with the doctor, is to protect the patient from unnecessary intervention and to care for her well-being.

TRUE INFORMED CONSENT

Recognising the patient's right to informed consent is crucial to ethical medical practice. In so doing it safeguards the patient's right to be respected as a person and to have her personal goals and values given due weight by involving her in shared decision-making. To talk, therefore, of 'patient consent' rather than 'informed consent' is unsatisfactory because it does not necessarily mean that the patient is adequately aware of what she is consenting to. Mrs Margaret Wigley, whose case was described at the beginning of this book, may well have been asked whether she would like to try a new drug – 'We think it will do you some good' is a favourite evasive formula used by doctors – but she was not told that it was still under trial.

Informed consent, if properly understood and entered into in good faith by both sides, has several important functions. As far as patients are concerned, it enables them to retain their human dignity and integrity; it protects them from unnecessary or undesired treatment, and, in the case of research, it ensures that they freely volunteer their bodies, being neither manipulated nor coerced into a trial which they do not understand. As for doctors, the obligation sincerely to seek informed consent means that they cannot be seduced into playing God. It also forces them to scrutinise their own motives for seeking a patient's consent (particularly important when it is required for any kind of research study), and to pay due regard to their patients' feeling and needs.

The doctrine of informed consent is also vitally important for society as a whole. As we saw in chapter 2, it enables the lay public to feel more confident about coming forward and expressing an opinion on medical ethical issues of concern to us all. It also reassures us that doctors are observing the wider community ethic outside their own codes which we will be examining in the next chapter.

Informed consent enables us to say no as well as yes.

4 Codes and laws

It is human nature that rules the world, not governments and regimes.

Svetlana Alliluyeva, *Observer* interview

HIPPOCRATES AT HELSINKI

For more than 2,000 years the medical profession has followed a code of conduct based on the homilies of Hippocrates, a remarkable Greek physician who established a school of medicine on Cos in the fifth century BC. The familiar maxim, 'Do no harm', is probably one of the most quoted tags of all time, as much by lay people as by doctors, and almost in the manner of an incantation – if I say, and you believe, I do no harm, then I will do no harm. Although much of the fabled Hippocratic Oath no longer has any relevance in a modern context, certain essential precepts still apply: the duty to act in the best interests of the patient, the duty to respect life and the duty to preserve the patient's confidence have all been incorporated in the World Medical Association's Declaration of Geneva (see Appendix A).

The Hippocratic tradition is also responsible for the strong emphasis that doctors have always placed on their standards of behaviour towards each other. As recently as 1982 I heard a doctor, invited to speak at a symposium about informed consent, proclaim his belief that medical ethics is medical etiquette. Needless to say, he had nothing useful to contribute to the topic under discussion.

The first modern attempt to update medical ethics was made by a Manchester physician, Thomas Percival, who in 1803 wrote his

Medical Ethics: or, a Code of Institutes and Precepts adapted to the Professional Conduct of Physicians and Surgeons, which he based on the upbringing of his own children. He recommended to doctors that 'They should study, also, in their deportment, so to unite tenderness with steadiness, and condescension with authority, as to inspire the minds of their patients with gratitude, respect and confidence.' Other codes followed, notably William Beaumont's code in 1833, which was the first to specify the duties of a doctor towards a patient on whom he is conducting an experiment, and in 1856 the Personal Code of Claude Bernard, described as the founder of experimental medicine, which stated among other things: 'that the principle of medical morality consists then in never performing on man an experiment which could be harmful to him in any degree whatsoever though the result may be of great interest to science, that is, of benefit to save the health of others.' The American Medical Association has been updating its code regularly since its first appearance in 1846, and recently the British Medical Association has been doing the same. Following the Declaration of Geneva, the World Medical Association has produced several more important Declarations relating to specific issues in medicine (see Appendix A). And there are many other codes which have been drawn up by national medical associations and other organisations with medical connections.

This plethora of codes suggests, quite correctly, that doctors have always been keenly conscious of the need to scrutinise their conduct and to behave in a manner which justifies their patients' confidence. The weakness common to them all is that they have been drawn up by the profession with no outside consultation. They are doctor-centred rather than patient-centred. The medical profession has always considered itself the most appropriate, indeed the only proper source, for defining its own ethics and setting its own standards – a view which, as we shall see later in this chapter, is wholeheartedly endorsed by another exclusive brotherhood, the British legal profession. Any hint of interference or disagreement, and doctors dance up and down in outrage. They claim that their medical training and the judgement of their peers gives them a special, indeed unique, right to determine their own rules and to regulate their members. The obvious problem with this claim is that it sets doctors apart from the general run of humanity when it comes to deciding the grounds on which they base their ethical decisions. As Ian Kennedy pointed out in one of his Reith lectures, '... they seem to operate on some form of automatic pilot when it comes to matters of ethics. We must gain their attention and provide the correct navigation.'

Easier said than done. When the Ombudsman was appointed in 1973, one of the areas specifically excluded from his brief was any investigation of actions taken in connection with diagnosis or the care and treatment of patients, provided that this action could be shown by the doctors concerned to be entirely based on clinical judgement. But often there is a fine, verging on invisible, line between clinical and ethical judgement. How, for example, does a doctor justify the all-too-common practice of offering an abortion to a woman only if she accepts sterilisation at the same time? There is an element of moral coercion here which cannot easily be explained away by an appeal to clinical expedience. More recently the Community Health Councils won parliamentary support for the right to institute complaints procedures, a right which was accepted in principle by the Secretary of State for Social Services in 1979 but has never been put into practice. It is naturally being strongly resisted by the medical lobby. The view that patients have rights too has hardly gained an inch in this country, at least not where it would make a real difference – inside the medical establishment. Yet in America a Patient's Bill of Rights was formulated as long ago as 1973, and the European Parliament has recently voted a resolution for something along the same lines (see chapter 9 for more discussion).

The codes so far examined have all, with the exception of Beaumont and Bernard, been related to general medical practice. After the Second World War and the Nuremberg revelations, both doctors and the world woke up to the horrors that had been committed in the name of science. The Nazi criminals pleaded in their defence that they were doing no more than had been done by many doctors before them, and in some respects they were right. Uncontrolled and often horribly painful experiments had been flourishing for years, as is testified by some gruesome accounts in the medical literature.*

The Nuremberg Code was formulated as part of the War Crimes Tribunal's judgement, and it is the first serious attempt to produce a universal code of conduct for doctors and scientists engaged in medical research involving human experimentation. It forms the basis

* See under chapter references

for all subsequent codes, most notably the World Medical Association's Declaration of Helsinki, first issued in 1964 and subsequently considerably revised in 1975 (see Appendix A). Both these codes take as their basic premise the view that medical progress is desirable and that doctors have a duty to do all in their power to improve their treatments while at the same time protecting their patients from undesirable or harmful interventions. Further, since scientific advance involves research which almost always includes some experimentation on human subjects, the volunteers must be truly volunteers and must be fully aware of what they are undertaking. These are unimpeachable moral assumptions. The question we have to ask is how well do these codes match their own high standards of moral probity? Or are they asking the impossible?

As we have seen, the first principle of the Nuremberg Code is an unequivocal statement of the doctrine of informed consent. In addition to insisting on the individual's 'free power of choice', it specifies exactly how much the volunteer should be told about the experiment so 'as to enable him to make an understanding and enlightened decision'. Some of the other principles are, however, so imprecisely worded as to be dangerous in their applications. Take, for instance, principle two which states that 'the experiment should be such as to yield fruitful results for the good of society, unprocurable by other methods or means of study, and not random and unnecessary in nature', or principle six which proposes that 'the degree of risk to be taken should never exceed that determined by the humanitarian importance of the problem to be solved by the experiment'. Phrases like 'good of society' or 'humanitarian importance' are wide open to subjective interpretation, and in the hands of an over-enthusiastic or unscrupulous investigator could be twisted to mean almost anything. Nor are there any recommendations to researchers to discuss their experimental project with their colleagues or, better still, refer it to an independent arbitrator. One thing is quite clear: although there is a clear prescription that patients and volunteers should be told about the experiment – its aims as well as what it involves – and their agreement obtained, there is absolutely no suggestion that doctors should explain why they think the experiment is necessary. This was, of course, 1947. Doctors themselves could not envisage then how complex the modern clinical trial was to become. So it is not surprising that the authors of this code restricted themselves to emphasising the importance of patients' consent rather than considering the details of the type of treatment that might be proposed.

The Declaration of Helsinki (1964 version) is a much more determined attempt to define the specific duties of medical researchers in the light of the more organised methods of research which were then evolving, exemplified by the development of controlled clinical trials. This code emphasises the fundamental distinction between therapeutic trials – those which offer a direct benefit to the patient involved – and non-therapeutic research which is purely scientific and offers no direct benefit to the subject. It outlines five basic principles for researchers, all of which are concerned with methodology. Consent is advised in the first type of trial, 'if at all possible, consistent with patient psychology', and in the case of incapacity it 'should also be procured from the legal guardian'. Much more emphasis is laid on the importance of obtaining uncoerced informed consent in the second type of trial where the volunteer is being asked to participate for purely altruistic reasons.

Although it was a valuable move in the right direction, doctors themselves obviously thought that this code was not sufficiently specific, for in 1975 they produced a revised and considerably expanded version. The Mark II Declaration of Helsinki (actually drawn up in Tokyo) is a remarkable document. Lucid and comprehensive, it covers practically all the issues raised by biomedical research, and if it were to be conscientiously observed by doctors and researchers, then patients and volunteers would have little to worry about.

The five basic principles have been extended to twelve, of which no fewer than four are concerned to define not merely what constitutes an informed consent but how it is to be obtained. The principles relating to procedures are also much more specific and they include the important new proviso (principle two) that both 'the design and performance of each experimental procedure involving human subjects should be clearly formulated in an experimental protocol which should be transmitted to a specially appointed independent committee for consideration, comment and guidance.' It also restates in much more vigorous terms where ultimate responsibility lies. From attributing it somewhat blandly in 1964 to the 'research worker' in the section on non-therapeutic research, the updated version apportions this responsibility to the *medically qualified* investigator alone and includes it as one of the twelve basic principles for all types of biomedical research, not just non-therapeutic trials. Finally, and possibly most important of all, this code stresses and repeats twice (in different words) the moral imperative that 'Concern for the interests of the subject must always prevail over the interests of science and society.'

Not surprisingly, many doctors are finding this code a hard saying. While they protest their respect for the ideals it holds out to them, they insist that in practice it is often impossible to follow, and they lean heavily on the get-out clause (number five in the section on medical research combined with professional care), which states that 'if the doctor considers it essential not to obtain informed consent, the specific reasons for this proposal should be stated in the experimental protocol for transmission to the independent committee.' This exemption is called 'therapeutic privilege', and the reasons and occasions for its application will be discussed in chapter 8.

All in all the Declaration of Helsinki covers most aspects of the moral issues arising out of biomedical research. There are, however, some notable gaps. For instance, it does not give guidelines for deciding how or indeed whether certain categories of volunteers, such as prisoners, children and the mentally handicapped, should be included in non-therapeutic research. It does not discuss the terms of volunteering; whether payment, for instance, or remission of sentence is permissible, nor does it give any guidance on the constitution of the independent arbitrating review committees. For example, should it be obligatory to have a lay person acting as the patient-representative on such a body? These omissions are to some extent justified by the caveat that 'the standards as drafted are only a guide to physicians all over the world. Doctors are not relieved from criminal, civil and ethical responsibilities under the laws of their own countries.'

This caution serves as a useful reminder of both the function and the limitations of any code of ethics. A code is neither legally binding nor does it make formal rules; it simply states principles and offers guidelines for action. Its value lies in being flexible and dynamic, open to change and review as the issues with which it is concerned themselves change or develop. The last forty years have seen extraordinary advances in medical treatment and methods of research; progress in some fields has been so rapid that it has caught doctors off guard as much as anyone else. The importance of a code like the Declaration of

Helsinki is that it reflects the 'best' current societal thinking on moral issues and relates it to the particular practical problems encountered by the profession, but there is nothing to prevent it from modifying its precepts or introducing new ones as medical expertise continues to develop, bringing new moral problems in its wake. The British medical profession is no more obliged than any other national group to observe the recommendations of the Declaration of Helsinki to the letter; doctors, scientists and anyone else involved with research – funding it, planning it, publishing results and so on – are merely urged to bear them in mind.

However, no code's scope can extend beyond dealing with problems which already exist and trying to persuade the profession to whom it is addressed to conform to its advice. *In vitro* fertilisation is a classic example of a situation where, as a result of brilliant research backed up by technological wizardry, entirely new ethical problems are emerging, some actual, some which can only be foreseen, but whose implications are so far ranging that society has decided they must not be left to the doctors to resolve on their own. The Warnock Committee, set up at the invitation of the Conservative government and led by the philosopher Dame Mary Warnock, published its important recommendations in July 1984 on this subject, among them the proposal that there should be a statutory licensing body chaired by a non-medical, non-scientific lay person and with substantial lay membership to supervise infertility services and research. Other recommendations include the   banning of surrogate motherhood agencies and the placing of a fourteen-day limit on research with embryos. Predictably, this report has aroused considerable controversy, and dissent, but this is entirely healthy and very welcome. We must hope, indeed insist, that this bold incursion into the hitherto fenced-off world of medical ethics is followed by similar enquiries into other fields of medical research.

In 1963 the Medical Research Council, an independent and highly respected research institution, published a document entitled *Responsibility in Investigations on Human Subjects* which is still regarded today as the prime authoritative guide for doctors engaged in research. Like the Declaration of Helsinki it clearly distinguishes between therapeutic and non-therapeutic clinical trials, but where it differs considerably is in not assigning any particular value to obtaining informed consent in the first kind of study. Providing the novel treatment under study is intended to benefit the patient in some way, then doctors are permitted to assume that patients have given their consent as they would if there were only one treatment available. The concession 'That it is both considerate and prudent to obtain the patient's agreement before using a novel procedure is no more than a requirement of good medical practice' may satisfy doctors but hardly meets our understanding of informed consent or indeed the basic principles of the Declaration of Helsinki. It is highly significant that where the MRC document does stipulate, albeit in a very summary form, the conditions necessary for obtaining consent in a non-therapeutic study, it refers throughout to 'true' rather than 'informed' consent. The inference is irresistible: are we to assume from this that the patient consent which is implicitly assumed in the traditionally defined patient-doctor relationship is not a true consent?

Quite apart from these serious semantic defects, this document suffers from a severe case of professional hubris. Following a gracious admission that 'moral codes are formulated by man', it proceeds to declare sternly that any changes which may be necessary to maintain their relevance can come only from the profession itself which must be eternally vigilant and self-disciplined. Nothing wrong with the admonition: it is the behaviour we expect from doctors. What is questionable is the assumption that the profession is supremely and uniquely empowered to determine its own standards of ethical behaviour. Interestingly, up to the time of writing this book, the MRC has not seen fit to revise its statement.

The British Medical Association publishes a *Handbook of Medical Ethics* which it updates from time to time. It has two paragraphs on 'Consent to Treatment', bits of which have been lifted wholesale from the MRC document; the rest is bland and fairly unhelpful. A comment like 'Doctors offer advice but it is the patient who decides whether or not to accept the advice' is an expense of meaning in a waste of words because it simply is not what happens in most NHS interactions between patient and doctor. Furthermore, for something purporting to be an ethical guide it is remarkably short on definitions or statements of principles. Controlled clinical trials also get the two-paragraph treatment, and no distinction is made between the two types of research. In one respect, though, the authors have shown a little more nerve. They actually recommend that consent must be obtained from the individual subjects and go so far as to specify that 'it should be obtained before randomisation if that is part of the method'. What they do not make clear is whether the doctor has to explain the randomisation procedure. Since this is a major stumbling block for most doctors, such imprecision can only encourage them to continue in their benevolent evasions (see chapters 5 and 6 for an explanation of randomisation and the problems it causes).

Given the paucity of advice available to them, we cannot really be surprised that most British doctors display ostrich tendencies on the subject of informed consent: if they do not talk about it too much, they hope it will go away. Although there is not much to admire in the way the Americans deliver their system of medical care – cakes for the rich, dry crusts for the poor – we could learn quite a lot from their high-minded and praiseworthy endeavours to resolve some of the major ethical issues arising out of research with human beings.

The Belmont Report is the result of a four-year enquiry, funded by the federal government, into the ethical principles which should govern such research, and it provides lucidly argued and well-defined guidelines.* The eleven members of the National Commission for the Protection of Human Subjects of Biomedical and Behavioral Research (three women and eight men) were distinguished representatives of several disciplines –medicine, law, theology, psychology and philosophy – and they consulted many experts and specialists in the course of their deliberations, all of whose reports have also been published for public consumption by the American equivalent of Her Majesty's Stationery Office. It is hard to imagine the British Medical Association (BMA) or the General Medical Council (GMC) or any of the august Royal medical colleges opening their doors so welcomingly to the outside world or even thinking of co-operating with each other in a similar venture. If anything, that possibility has now become even more remote since the English courts have firmly declared that they hold no brief for American legal opinion on informed consent.

PROTECTION OR DEFENCE?

Common law is the unwritten law of England. It is based on a widely accepted community ethic which has become endorsed by long-standing usage. As we know, the legal doctrine of informed consent

* See chapter references

has emerged comparatively recently, but the idea that a person's bodily integrity should be protected from unauthorised touching or invasion has very ancient antecedents in English law going right back to the Middle Ages. It was not, however, until 1767 that a patient brought an action against his doctors alleging that he had not consented to a particular treatment. On that occasion the judge stated: 'It is reasonable that a patient should be told what is about to be done to him, that he may take courage and put himself in such a situation as to enable him to undergo the operation.'*

As the principle of self-determination took root in our culture, eventually to be declared a human right, so the laws of the land gradually embodied this right in various enactments. The need for patient consent to surgical operations was recognised at the beginning of this century when consent forms became a statutory requirement, but by an odd quirk this requirement for the patient's signed consent has not been extended to drug treatment which can be just as invasive.

By comparison with the flood of malpractice suits invoking informed consent in North America, the British incidence is a mere trickle and one which may well dry up altogether, given the nature of some recent judgements which have made it clear that the British courts consistently prefer to opt for the 'professional standard' rather than a 'patient standard' when it comes to deciding how much information a doctor should disclose. One of the most important cases to state this principle is the *Bolam* v. *Friern Hospital Management Committee*, already mentioned in chapter 3.

Many of these cases have been characterised by a great deal of intricate legal wrangling as to whether a charge of non-consent can be brought under an action for battery (unlawful touching) or negligence (the doctor's failure in his or her duty of care). The distinction was finally established in 1980 in the *Chatterton* v. *Gerson* case. The plaintiff, a Miss Elizabeth Chatterton, had been suffering from chronic intractable pain following a hernia operation. She agreed to a second operation to block off a sensory nerve; unfortunately, not only did it fail to relieve her pain but it also left her with one permanently numb leg. She complained that the surgeon had failed to inform her of this risk, but her case was dismissed on the grounds that 'once the patient is

---

* *Slater* v. *Baker and Stapleton*, 94 ER 860

informed in broad terms of the nature of the procedure which is intended, and gives her consent, that consent is real, and the cause of the action on which to base a claim for failure to go into risks and implications is negligence, not trespass.' The judge did add that 'getting the patient to sign a proforma expressing consent to undergo the operation "the effect and nature of which have been explained to me," as was done here . . . should be a valuable reminder to everyone of the need for explanation and consent.'

Negligence is a much more difficult action to bring than battery because even if fault can be proved and the patient has sustained injuries which justify the action, she will get compensation only for those damages which could have been predicted as a consequence of the doctor's negligence. Although damages for unforeseen medical complications are allowed under a charge of battery, they are not recoverable in a charge of negligence. This narrow view of what constitutes actionable negligence creates a host of problems for the patient. Not only does she have to find expert witnesses who will back up her claim that she was inadequately informed about the material risks, but they must also support her contention that the injury she suffered could have been predicted. Finding doctors who are prepared to testify against their own colleagues is the first and major hurdle to overcome, as anyone who has tried to bring such an action will bitterly corroborate. Even if these witnesses are willing to say that the doctor in question was negligent, getting them to agree that he or she could and should have foreseen the unfortunate consequences is almost impossible except in the most flagrantly obvious cases.

Where it is consent rather than treatment that is at issue, the whole thing becomes, for the aggrieved patient, a nightmare of conflicting opinions about what constitutes adequate disclosure of information. The medical consensus (upheld by the law in this country but not in North America) is that the patient has a right to be told only about those risks which are reasonably probable and serious in their consequences. Remote risks do not need to be revealed, and if a doctor believes that telling the patient too much about possible complications would cause her undue distress, then he or she is perfectly entitled to withhold it. In effect, *the patient will be told only what the doctors think it is fit for her to know, not what she might consider necessary to make an informed decision for herself.* This outrageous paternalism has been endorsed in case after case in the English courts where judges have unfailingly maintained that the only standard which counts for assessing the amount of information to be disclosed is the standard 'upheld by a substantial body of medical opinion, and that this body of medical opinion is both respectable and responsible, and experienced in this particular field of medicine'.*

The idea that the patient as a reasonable person might justifiably consider her own standard to be at least as (if not more so) valid and relevant as 'a practice rightly accepted as proper by a body of skilled and experienced medical men', was thus roundly dismissed by the Master of the Rolls, Sir John Donaldson, in the most recent case to come to the Court of Appeal (*Sidaway* v. *the Board of Governors of Bethlem Royal Hospital* 1984). This case is deeply disturbing in its implications on a number of counts and therefore merits closer examination.

First, the evidence and the judgement. The patient, Mrs Amy Sidaway, was not told by her neuro-surgeon in 1974 that the operation he advised to relieve her of severe and persistent pain in her neck and shoulder was elective; that is, she did not have to have it but it might do the trick. Nor did he tell her that there was a one to two per cent risk that her spinal cord might be damaged. In the event, it was damaged, disabling Mrs Sidaway so severely that her damages were estimated at £67,000. The grounds for her action were that the doctor whom she described as 'a man of very, very few words' had not told her of this risk, and that if she had known of it she would have refused the operation. The judge conceded her claim was true but dismissed it, saying that she had no case in law because she had been told as much 'in 1974 [as] would have been accepted as proper by a responsible body of skilled and experienced neuro-surgeons'.

Second, the implications of this judgement which was whole-heartedly supported by the two other judges. The doctrine of informed consent in medicine was rejected as being 'no part of English law' (Lord Justice Dunn) and should not be extended 'outside the field of property rights' (Lord Justice Browne-Wilkinson). The medical standard was firmly upheld as being superior to any other standard, either the patient's or what might be deemed objectively fair in a court of law. All three judges firmly rejected the Canadian opinion (confirmed in *Reibl* v. *Hughes* in 1980) that 'the patient's right to know

* Justice Hirst in *Hills* v. *Potter and Another* 1983

what risks are involved in undergoing or foregoing certain surgery or other treatment' should be considered and that expert medical evidence, although relevant, was not conclusive in determining the degree of adequate disclosure. In one breath the Master of the Rolls declared that the 'law would not permit the medical profession to play God' and in the next said that all was well so long as doctors abided by their own 'rightly' accepted practices. Lord Justice Dunn permitted himself to surmise that it was not paternalism to reject the doctrine of informed consent since it was a feature of the doctor-patient relationship in this country that most patients 'preferred to put themselves unreservedly in the hands of their doctors'. Furthermore, he warned that if the court were to accept Mrs Sidaway's claim, then the floodgates would be opened to similar claims of negligence and doctors would become more concerned with safeguarding themselves than with looking after their patients. At the time of writing, the case of this unfortunate woman, who is now in her seventies, is pending a final appeal to the House of Lords, but if the opinion of the *British Medical Journal*'s legal correspondent is anything to go by (and his relief at the verdict is undisguised – 288 pp. 802-3) then it is unlikely that their Lordships in the House will contradict their peers in the Court of Appeal.

The British medical profession is profoundly nervous that the spectre of frivolous malpractice suits, which undoubtedly haunts their American colleagues, will cross the Atlantic. But who, one is obliged to ask, is the law protecting and who is it defending? It seems a peculiar way to go about protecting the rights of the individual if those rights can be set aside any time a powerful professional group cries 'foul' because the rules it has made for its own conduct, and without any outside consultation, are challenged. Defensive medicine as it is practised in the States is, largely because of a number of ill-thought-out and contradictory legal judgements in various states, undoubtedly a scourge and not something we would wish our doctors to be obliged to emulate. Yet surely it is not beyond the wit of reasonable women and men to arrive at an acceptable and honourable compromise such as appears to happen in Canada where patients are allowed to take responsibility for themselves and their decisions? Doctors may be jubilant now but I doubt that the Sidaway case has finally scotched informed consent, although it has certainly suffered a serious reverse.

It needs only one patient to bring a similar action in relation to a controlled clinical trial to stir up a real hornet's nest, and when that happens doctors will find it much harder to defend their policy of benevolent concealment, given what they have prescribed for themselves in their own codes of conduct. As we saw in chapter 1, it could have happened in 1982.

Part two
Limits to science

There must be some barriers that are not to be crossed, some limits fixed, beyond which people must not be allowed to go. The very existence of morality depends upon it.

Dame Mary Warnock, *The Warnock Report*

5 Randomised controlled clinical trials

In a controlled trial, as in all experimental work, there is no need in the search for precision to throw common sense out of the window.
Sir Austin Bradford Hill, *Medical Ethics and Controlled Trials*

THE SCIENTIFIC ART

For Hippocrates and his followers who knew next to nothing about anatomy and physiology and even less about the causes of disease, medicine was an Art. They believed that to be in good health was to be living in a state of harmony with nature. Disease, like life, was a process governed by natural laws which must be closely observed and the symptoms treated appropriately in order to restore the balance between the sick person and her or his environment. Medicines were secondary to diet and exercise and patients were encouraged to co-operate with their doctors so that together they might conquer the disease. What these early doctors lacked in scientific knowledge they made up for by setting an example of how to practise careful, observant clinical medicine which has always been emulated by conscientious doctors, has been ignored at the patient's peril, and is now seeing a revival in modern holistic medicine which emphasises that it is good science as well as humane medicine to treat the whole person, mind and spirit as well as body.

Taking a leap through the ages and ignoring some interesting advances by later Greeks in anatomy and surgery and isolated pockets of civilised practice like those at Salerno and in the schools of Arabian medicine which combined Eastern influences with the old Hippocratic tradition, medicine, in common with other disciplines, sank into the mists of barbarism and superstition. It was not until the Renaissance and the discovery of the ancient classical writings that the medical profession began to liberate itself from the sterile dogmatism which it had acquired from its close association with the Church.

The spirit of scientific enquiry reawakened and the birth of modern scientific medicine can be given a precise date. It occurred in 1628 when William Harvey published his discovery of the circulation of the blood. This was a landmark achievement in the history of scientific discovery, and also heralded a new direction in medicine. Harvey demonstrated by his painstaking investigation of animals and human subjects the need to test a scientific hypothesis by an orderly accumulation of facts and then use the evidence thus supplied to make rigorous logical deductions.

Harvey's appreciation of scientific method for testing theories took a long time taking root. Although he was followed by many other brilliant doctor-researchers who employed similar methods to make important discoveries about bodily structures and functions, and some who began to enquire into the causes of disease (aetiology) and the process of disease (epidemiology), the great majority of doctors continued to practise along traditional lines, allowing intuition – some would say wishful thinking – and their limited clinical observation to guide them in their choice of treatments. It was not until the nineteenth century that experimental medicine began to be considered as justifiable, indeed essential, if there was to be any real progress in medical practice.

Judged by today's standards, the early trials were distressingly haphazard, but they could nonetheless be wonderfully effective – as was the study of infection performed by Lister's precursor, a Hungarian doctor, Ignaz Semmelweiss, in 1857. He had noticed that the deadly puerperal fever was more common among women who had been examined by medical students than by midwives. Noting that the students had come straight from dissecting cadavers, he made them soak their hands in a disinfecting solution before examining the patients, and the death rate dropped dramatically from 18 per cent to 1.2 per cent.

New treatments were proliferating and it became increasingly apparent to the more scientifically minded members of the profession that clinical observation and judgement, although valuable, was too easily distorted by prejudice and personal bias to be reliable. What was needed was some more objective method of verification. The first trial by numbers was done in the early nineteenth century by a Frenchman, Professor Pierre-Charles-Alexandre Louis, who was able to demonstrate the uselessness of blood-letting by comparing the results of large numbers of cases.*

However, it was not until well into this century that controlled clinical trials began to be accepted as a method of scientific evaluation. And it was not until after the Second World War that the principle of randomisation was introduced into clinical research. This concept of random allocation was described by its innovator, the statistician Sir Ronald Fisher, who first used it in studies of agricultural crop production, as the primary principle of experimental design. It was another eminent statistician, Sir Austin Bradford Hill, who initiated its use in medical research with the historic trial in 1946 of the antibiotic Streptomycin for tuberculosis. Very simply, randomisation operates on the 'toss of a coin' principle: subjects suffering from a particular illness at the same stage are randomly allocated to different groups for different treatments and then carefully observed and followed up to compare the results. Its purpose is to eliminate any element of human or accidental bias in selecting patients for treatment which would distort the assessment of the results. Clinical trials using this principle of randomisation are called randomised controlled trials – RCTs as they will be referred to from now on in this book.

That RCTs have become so widely used is probably due as much as anything to the pithy monograph extolling their virtues written by Dr Archibald Cochrane in the early seventies.† He advocated not merely that they were efficient for testing new treatments but that they provided a cost-effective method for testing traditional procedures, many of them outdated and illogical, which the NHS was finding difficulty in discarding. He urged that even simple

---

* His conclusions were largely ignored; bloodletting with leeches was still going on in the 1930s. (Geoffrey Beattie, 'Once upon a time a leech survived the patient', the *Guardian*, 21 April 1984)

† See chapter reference

measures, like when a patient should be got out of bed after surgery, should be put to the test by this rigorous method.

Since then RCTs have been considerably developed and refined and they are now extensively used to test new drugs, surgical techniques, radiotherapy, screening procedures, alternative methods of delivering medical care and a host of other medical interventions. This means that although only a relatively small percentage of patients actually receiving medical treatment are doing so in a trial (approximately 10 per cent), there are many more of us drawn from the so-called healthy population who may be involved in a trial, with or without our knowledge. For example, a trial testing different methods of counteracting hypertension or a new way of offering a screening service, say for cervical cancer, can be done on a regional basis throughout the community. Very often in such trials neither of the comparison groups taken out of a selected population will be aware that they are being monitored in a study.

RCTs arouse strong emotions in the medical profession. They have their enthusiastic proponents who are convinced that they are the only effective way to validate new and old treatments. They also have their detractors and doubters who are concerned about them both for methodological reasons and for their ethical implications. The RCT, with its emphasis on precise measurement, is undoubtedly one of the developments in medicine which has edged it closer than it has ever been to the status of an exact science. But now it is also more timely than ever to remember the warning paradox voiced by Bertrand Russell that 'all exact science is dominated by the idea of approximation.' The practice of medicine will remain an art as well as a science for as long as human beings remain human and do not allow themselves to be robotomised by their own technology.

HUMAN EXPERIMENTATION

Few people would seriously argue that doctors are wrong to want to increase their understanding of the human body and the ills to which it is prone. Doctors want to be able to do the best they can for their present patients and they would like to do even better for future patients. *We* want them to find the cure for cancer and other serious diseases and to help us to live longer and healthier lives. *We* expect them to give us the best available treatment. *We* want to feel safe in their hands, reassured that whatever they suggest to us is backed by sound scientific knowledge and that our welfare is their first consideration. We want it all, but medical advance is impossible without research and experimentation – and some of that experimentation must be done on human beings.

In a sense all medical treatment is experimental. However well tried a particular therapy may be, the doctor can never be entirely sure how the individual patient will respond. Far more experimental is any treatment which is offered to patients simply because the doctor believes it works, even though it may never have been put to the test in a comparison with a control group of patients who either are not getting the treatment or are being offered an alternative. Until not so very long ago, this is how doctors introduced all new therapies, and if they appeared effective then they would be incorporated into the orthodox canon of treatments taught in medical school. Incredibly, some patients are still suffering the legacy of this kind of uncontrolled experimentation today. For example, the classic radical Halsted operation for breast cancer which involves extended and mutilating surgery was, for more than eighty years, thought to be the only method for dealing with this disease. It was not until the fifties that a few doctors, realising that the mortality rates were not improving, began to question its value and set up controlled clinical trials to compare it with less drastic forms of mastectomy. (The exception was Sir Geoffrey Keynes, who in the thirties tried radiotherapy instead and found, by comparing his results with those of orthodox surgery, that it worked at least as well in terms of survival and spared his patients a lot of misery.) Today, the surgeons in this country who persist in doing the Halsted operation can probably be counted on the fingers of one hand (in America it remains a popular method), but in this as in other areas of medical practice there are still numbers of dinosaur doctors who apparently neither read their journals nor listen to their colleagues and continue to use similar, sometimes discredited procedures. Their opposite numbers – the lemming breed – are quite as alarming because they will eagerly try out new treatments which may still be under trial, arguing that they look good enough to them and that therefore it would be unethical to withhold them.

Under controlled conditions there are three kinds of human experimentation. First there is the non-therapeutic trial which is carried out on healthy volunteers who will get no personal benefit from the experiment but who offer their bodies, or their minds, to test a hypothesis, the effects of a drug or perhaps a psychological theory. The second form of human experimentation, or study, as doctors prefer to call it, is that done on patients with a particular illness or condition in clinical trials to compare the merits of different treatments. This type of clinical research combined with professional care enables doctors who are genuinely uncertain about which treatment they should be offering to their patients to feel secure that those who get the new treatment will be carefully monitored and that the final judgement of the results does not rely on their opinion alone. Finally, there is a subclass of experimentation in which patients who are being treated for one condition may also act as controls for patients receiving a trial treatment for some other condition. (A control group of patients in a clinical trial receives the 'best standard therapy' and is used as a measure of comparison with another group of patients allotted to the new treatment under study.)

- Provided that the patients or volunteers who participate in all these types of experiments are fully informed and freely give their consent, they are not being used as guinea pigs.
- Provided that the trials are well designed and conform to the conditions prescribed in the Declaration of Helsinki, they are a reliable and ethical way of conducting medical research.
- Provided that the doctors who participate in a trial always put the welfare of their individual patients before the interests of science and society, they can be sure that they are caring for their patients according to the highest medical and ethical standards.

These three provisos are fundamentally important in the ethical conduct of any trial using human subjects and they should be equally well understood by both categories of participants – patients/volunteers and doctors.

Underlying these stipulations there are three important questions that have to be asked about any trial, not when it is all over but before it ever gets launched: Is it essential? Is it effective? Is it ethical? If the answer is 'no' to either the first or second question, it will certainly be 'no' to the third as well. Bad science in medical research is definitely immoral. An ill-conceived or unnecessary trial is an inexcusable waste of people, resources and time and can have serious, possibly disastrous consequences for the future. Even if the answer is 'yes' to the first and second questions on scientific grounds, it may still be 'no' to the third. Good science is not necessarily good ethics.

Before we consider the overall ethical implications of trials both good and bad (see chapter 6), we need to know what consistutes a good trial (the RCT in particular) and what it can be expected to achieve; concomitantly, we need to understand what factors can make a good trial go bad . . . 'there's many a slip 'twixt cup and lip.'

PLANNING THE PROTOCOL

The protocol is the detailed medical instruction which sets out the objectives of the trial and explains in precise terms the strategy that participating doctors must adhere to throughout the trial – such matters as the criteria for selecting patients, how the treatments are to be administered and how the patients should be followed up. Other points that must be carefully considered at the planning stage and written into the protocol are the type of data to be collected, the methods to be used and how such data are to be analysed. This is an exhaustive, time-consuming process which can take months, sometimes years, and may involve a small pilot study to test the feasibility of doing a trial at all. Planning should be done by a team of specialists rather than a single doctor to ensure that every detail is checked and counter-checked.

A key member of the planning team is the statistician who ought to be brought in right at the beginning of the project to discuss the stated aims, advise on their viability and, if necessary, suggest modifications without losing sight of the ultimate medical objectives. The statistician's most important function is to ensure that the correct technical procedures are observed throughout the trial. These include measuring the results and helping the medical investigators to evaluate and interpret them as they emerge, a process which again may take years before a final conclusion can be reached. Obviously the statistician is not qualified to assess the medical merits of the treatments under trial; her or his crucial responsibility is to make certain that no statistical errors creep into either the design of the trial or its evaluation, for, undetected, these could lead the investigators to misread the evidence.

RUNNING A RANDOMISED CONTROLLED TRIAL (RCT)

Take a trial which has been designed to test a new anti-cancer drug. Before the drug can even be considered for a controlled clinical trial it will have been carefully tested in laboratory and animal tests. If it looks good at this stage it will then be offered to patients for whom all other treatments have failed. Only if it shows definite results after this second stage can it be studied in a clinical trial. Promise, however, is not good enough; it must also satisfy the investigators that the risk of hazardous side effects is not going to outweigh its benefits. Immediately a problem arises: not all side effects can be foreseen and often their presence may not emerge for some considerable time, so safeguards have to be written into the trial protocol making it possible to pick up adverse reactions quickly and allow participating doctors to exercise their own clinical judgement. For example, if a doctor becomes concerned about the effects of the drug on a particular patient, he must be able to withdraw that patient at once, and the patient too must know that she is free to withdraw at any time, for whatever reason. Although withdrawals from a trial make it more difficult to analyse the data, the problem is not insuperable so long as the possibility has been catered for in the trial protocol.

What now follows is a description of an RCT run along *ideal* lines. The researchers decide how many patients they will need to enter to obtain a significant result. Sample size is extremely important. Too many patients means you are involving subjects unnecessarily and increasing the costs, apart from making it more difficult to get the precise answers you are seeking. Too few patients means you will probably not get a valid result. It is vital to get an adequate sample size speedily in order to complete the trial and obtain results as soon as possible, so the researchers will hope to enlist widescale support from doctors, hospital-based clinicians, and/or GPs, depending on the type of study.

These multi-centre trials, some of them international, are run by a central administration which issues the protocol and the randomised instructions, collects and screens the data and deals with problems. Before doctors can enter the trial they must get approval of it from their own hospital ethical committee and they must themselves be morally and medically convinced that the trial is necessary because they consider they do not know which is the best therapy. In the course of their practice they then select those patients who are eligible to enter the trial because they share certain characteristics specified in the protocol; for example, they fall within a particular age group and they have the same stage and type of disease.

Before proceeding any further with an individual patient the doctor informs her about the trial and asks if she will agree to participate. How this should be done is clearly defined in Principle 9 of the Declaration of Helsinki:

> In any research on human beings, each potential subject must be adequately informed of the aims, methods, anticipated benefits and potential hazards of the study and the discomfort it may entail. He or she should be informed that he or she is at liberty to abstain from participation in the study and that he or she is free to withdraw his or her consent to participation at any time. The doctor should then obtain the subject's freely-given informed consent, preferably in writing.

Randomisation is an essential element of the trial procedure so the patient must understand what this will mean if she gives her consent: neither she nor her doctor will know in advance which treatment she is going to get because her treatment will be randomly allocated to her by the computer at the trial centre. She must also understand that she can change her mind and withdraw her consent at any stage, which might mean as soon as she has been informed of the treatment allocation.

Trial patients are randomly allocated to two groups. Group A receives the new drug, perhaps in conjunction with the standard treatment, and Group B (the control group) receives the standard treatment. There are several variations on this basic theme. There may be more than two groups to test permutations of the treatment. The trial may be 'blind', which means that the patient does not know which treatment she is receiving, or it may be 'double blind', meaning that her doctor does not know either. The alternative to the new drug may be no treatment at all, or it may be a placebo in the form of a dummy drug. Double blind trials are mainly used to test drugs, and they are done in order to make doubly sure that doctors are not subconsciously biased in their opinion of the relative merits of the treatments. In a trial which is comparing two surgical procedures or a surgical procedure against a drug, it is plainly impossible to conceal the differences in treatment, at least from the doctor.

WHY RANDOMISE?

Randomisation has three major advantages for statistical analysis. First of all it guarantees that treatments are compared solely on their merits, and are not affected by any kind of personal bias by doctors in selecting patients, whether conscious or not. This is possible only if doctors abide by the rules of the protocol and assess and register all the patients who are eligible immediately they come into their care, not after they have had some time to think about their treatment.

Secondly, and *only if* the trial has enough subjects, randomisation reduces the chance of an accidental bias creeping in because of some variable among patients – say a major difference in the development of their disease – which was not foreseen as important at the time of defining the characteristics of patients eligible for the trial. The 'only if' matters because in a small trial this variable will almost certainly cause an excessive imbalance, whereas with adequate numbers this variable can be safely presumed to have been randomised into the treatment groups, thus keeping the treatments truly comparable.

Finally, randomisation makes it possible to do a valid significance test of the treatments because it is based on the principle that any of the patients in any of the groups could have received any one of the treatments being compared. A 'significant difference' means that one of these treatments, measured by a predetermined level of significance (usually 5 per cent), shows a more favourable outcome than could have been expected on a random allocation of equally effective treatments.

This view that the treatments are equally effective is called a null hypothesis and it must be the starting point of any RCT. Apart from being sound logic it is also sound ethics. It is only the inherent neutrality of this null hypothesis that can justify the trial, because once a particular treatment has been proved to be significantly better than another it would obviously be highly unethical to submit it to any further comparison testing which would mean withholding it from some patients. Although conduct so blatantly unethical is improbable, something perilously close to this does happen when treatment comparisons are continually repeated in new trials. This may be because the new researchers profess themselves to be dissatisfied with the available evidence or because they are unaware that similar, possibly better-designed trials are already in progress. More questionably, it may be because they want to get their names on a piece of research.

Only if the investigators can sincerely postulate the null hypothesis will they be able to answer the first of the three questions which must be asked about any trial: is it essential? Yes, it is essential to test an unproven new treatment but only on condition that by the time it reaches the stage of a clinical trial the evidence shows that it is at least as good as the best standard therapy and no better, otherwise it would be unethical to withhold it.

Now for the second question. Is the RCT always and in all circumstances the best and most effective method for conducting valid medical research? Just to put this question is regarded as heresy in certain medical quarters where the RCT has acquired the status of received truth. There are others, however, including many doctors and researchers, who fear that its scientific advantages may have been overstated to the point of becoming a dogma and at the expense of other profoundly important values, human as well as medical.

PITFALLS AND PROBLEMS

The RCT poses a variety of problems for doctors which are scientific, ethical and psychological in nature. The psychological difficulties are perhaps the easiest to understand, although this does not make them any easier to resolve. For example, by allowing the computer to choose the treatment, doctors are going against a basic tenet of their training and tradition which is to reassure their patients that they are giving them personal, individualised care. They are obliged to surrender an important part of their clinical autonomy – that crucial moment at the beginning of treating a patient when the doctor confidently says 'I think the treatment you need is X' is denied to them. They fear that they will lose the patient's trust and faith in their competence by admitting, as they must if they ask a patient to enter a trial, that they do not know which treatment is best. Above all, they find it difficult – many would say it is impossible – to explain to their patients the cold, apparently inhuman logic behind randomisation.

Since the claims for the RCT's superiority are based on science, we need to examine these first and with yet more questions in mind. Are the claims justified? If they are not, then we need go no further, but if they are, or at least are sufficiently often to make them a valuable resource in medical research, then we have to ask: how can they be balanced with the ethical necessity not to use patients as means?

As we have already seen, taking a randomised sample allows the investigator to absorb the problem of unforeseen or uncontrollable variables emerging during the course of the trial which would distort the results. But absorbing the problem, or refusing to credit it with any importance, does not eliminate it and may, as one critic has pointed out, 'obscure, rather than illuminate, interactive effects between treatments and personal characteristics'.*

Talking about randomisation in the abstract tends to disguise its limitations. It is an essentially paradoxical concept. Its meaning is 'haphazard' or 'aimless', yet its effect is the reverse when it is applied as a principle of measurement in statistical research. Although it is a valuable precision tool for gauging defined, quantifiable facts, it is an extremely blunt instrument when it comes to making the qualitative assessments which are equally if not more necessary in medical research. Human beings are not like grains of wheat. They cannot be measured for single, simple reactions in the way that Fisher originally used the randomising principle to measure crop yields. They are infinitely varied in their histories and uniquely different in their responses, and these differences will inevitably affect the performance of the treatment they receive. However closely matched two groups of patients may be, they are never going to be identical and the differences between them (known and unknown) are likely to be more important than the crude similarities which have brought them together for the purposes of a trial.

Randomisation is limited in its scope because it can get its answer only by reducing the influence of variables. It therefore limits the scope of a trial by reducing the number of questions it can ask. An RCT does not necessarily ask how or why one treatment works better than another. It may not even be designed to ask whether and when the variations between treatments are important or trivial, although this information may be vitally important for future practice. It simply seeks to ascertain whether there is a significant difference, say of survival or length of remission, between two treatments for a particular class of patients. By concentrating on this aspect, the RCT investigators may ignore or discount other valuable indications about the treatments.

*   M.C. Weinstein, see chapter references

The RCT seeks certainty, but we do not have to be a philosopher or a scientist to know that the quest for complete certainty is an illusion The most the RCT can do is to establish an extra degree of reliability along the scale of enquiry between ignorance and certainty.* Nor is certainty, any more than quantifiability, the overriding goal of medical research. Although the RCT can be more certain about the simple evidence it provides, it may not always yield as rich a store of useful information as, for instance, a historical retrospective trial which relies on comparing the accumulated past evidence of the effects of different treatments on groups of patients. Even though patients in an historical trial will not have been rigorously categorised as in an RCT, careful observation and comparisons of experience still have a part to play in clinical medicine. Those who dismiss historical trials as too diffuse to yield more than unsubstantiated generalisations should perhaps remember Santayana's chastening reminder that 'those who cannot remember the past are condemned to repeat it'. Organised clinical observation in whatever form is always useful, even if it does no more than furnish a compelling reason for doing an RCT.

Further limitations which RCTs share with other types of clinical trial are that they neither produce the truth automatically nor are they as totally objective as some of their enthusiasts claim. Even if the statistical methods for evaluating the data are faultless, there still remains a strong element of subjectivity, both in choosing what is to be defined as significant and in selecting the aspects of the data to be analysed. Unless the investigators are super-scrupulous and hyper-objective when they come to interpret and report the results, there is a strong risk that they will be tempted to play down indications which might reduce the value of the significant difference; for instance, a drug which undoubtedly improves survival may impair the quality of that extra life by producing an undesirable side effect like impotence or extreme, disabling nausea which some patients might prefer not to suffer. They, and their doctors, must at least be allowed to know that the possibility exists, and to what degree, in order to decide for themselves what risks they are prepared to accept for what benefits.

RCTs are undoubtedly effective, providing that their limitations are accepted and properly understood. They are frequently, but not invariably, the best method for testing treatments. Up to now we have

* H.A.F. Dudley, see chapter references

considered only the technical problems they pose, and only in theory. The next chapter will consider their ethical implications for patients and the many administrative, psychological and ethical problems they present in practice to doctors.

6 Trials on trial

A study is ethical or not at its inception; it does not
become ethical because it turned up valuable data.
Henry K. Beecher, *Research and the Individual*

ARE THEY ETHICAL?

The answer must obviously be affirmative if we are to accept RCTs
in principle, but a positive response does not exempt us from
repeating the question each and every time a new trial is
proposed. Up to now those who have put this question have been
the experts – the medical researchers, the doctors contemplating
participation, ethical committees, lawyers and moral philosophers.
Spot the missing person in this group? Why, yes, it is the patient,
or potential patient – you and me. Without our participation a trial
cannot even start; without our consent it should not take place; yet
when has anyone asked us what we think either about the ethics
of trials, their aims and procedures, or the ethics of our
involvement?

In keeping with this book's underlying aim to redress the
prevailing imbalance in the patient-doctor relationship and restore
it to a more just equipoise between differing and sometimes
conflicting interests, I propose to reverse the conventional order of
discussion about the ethics of RCTs by the simple device of
considering them first from the patient's standpoint. Of course,
doctors have problems and to a great extent their problems are also the
patients' problems, but if patients do not understand what trials are
about and do not know the conditions of their participation, they are in
no position to judge their merits or their disadvantages.

In Part One we considered, and rejected on philosophical grounds, some of the more familiar arguments which doctors may use to support their view that it is impossible to obtain full or meaningful informed consent from patients. In Part Three we will re-evaluate these arguments in the light of the day-to-day interaction between patient and doctor and seek to propose some solutions which are both ethical and humane. But for present purposes our enquiry is restricted to the special problems engendered by the RCT's structure and methodology.

In some ways an RCT can be compared to an ambitious building scheme: the medical researchers who plan it are the architects; the statistician is the consulting engineer who enables them to make their design a practical reality, and the clinicians who participate in the trial are the craftsmen who lend their skills to its completion. So far so good, but it is at the point of patient entry that this analogy stops dead in its tracks. Although patients are the essential raw material for the project, they are also the sole reason for the project; it is for their benefit and theirs alone that the scheme exists. Patients are not bricks and mortar, objects which can be used or discarded without a second thought. Patients are people in exactly the same way as doctors, researchers and statisticians are people; therefore, to enter them as unwitting or inadequately informed participants into a trial is a dehumanising act which degrades those who do it as much as those who are being used as means to an end instead of as an end in themselves.

The principle of randomisation is the crucial feature which distinguishes an RCT from other types of clinical trial. In particular, the RCT is different from the so-called historical or retrospective trial which considers the data after the event by comparing two groups of patients who were selectively treated. The trouble with the historical trial is that there is no way of knowing what the differences are between the groups because they were neither matched nor randomised in the first place. Although randomisation is the most precise method for scientific measurement, it is neither easy to explain nor – and this is what counts for the patient – always easy to justify.

To see what this means in real terms we need to look at some examples. Starting with a simple one, consider the case of a drug which is being tested for its controlling qualities in a chronic, disabling illness like rheumatoid arthritis. The new drug is not capable of curing the condition but it may halt its progress or offer a significant measure of relief from pain. Plainly, patients would welcome it if it could be shown conclusively to be effective and free of dangerous or undesirable side effects. Since the drug is neither life-saving or even curative, it ought to be relatively uncomplicated for a doctor to explain to the patient why it needs to be tested in a controlled trial and why randomising it provides the surest method of assessment. Most people can readily grasp the point of randomisation in these circumstances and most would probably be willing to chance 'the luck of the draw' and enter the trial, providing they were reassured that if they did not get the new drug they would still be getting some form of conventional treatment.

Now take the case of a drug which is being tested for its adjuvant properties in the treatment of cancer. Adjuvant means that it is used as a back-up to the primary treatment of the tumour which may have been surgery or radiotherapy. Cancer is a life-threatening disease, so the introduction of a new drug, whether its aim is to eliminate the disease from the system or control its advance, will be supremely important for the individual patient. Even if the doctor explains quite truthfully that no one yet knows whether the drug works or whether it will produce unacceptable side effects, there are many patients who, finding themselves in this situation, would want to seize any opportunity of extra treatment, however uncertain its outcome. Objectively, they might be perfectly capable of understanding the advantages of randomisation, but subjectively they might be unable to accept it for themselves, given that it means they would have no more than a 50/50 chance of getting the new drug. Patients who feel like this cannot be entered into the trial, and if enough informed patients were to feel the same way, then the trial itself would obviously be in jeopardy.

The investigators are frustrated because the patient's refusal seems irrational and is hindering them in their efforts to make a medical advance. The patient herself may well appreciate that she is not behaving reasonably from a scientific standpoint – after all the new treatment she chooses may turn out to be worse not better than the old – and, should this be the case, it would be irrational of her to turn round and blame the doctors who had warned her of the possibility. What she can assert with perfect reason is that as an autonomous human being she must be allowed to make her own decisions, and take responsibility for them, even if they turn out to be mistakes.

As for the second 'scientific' objection that such patients are behaving selfishly towards future generations by denying them the chance to know for certain about a treatment: well, who is being irrational now? The first thought of a seriously ill patient is for herself and her survival, and there is nothing irrational about that. Can anyone reasonably expect such a person suddenly to be suffused with noble altruism towards the anonymous world beyond her bed? The investigators may not think that patients are being sacrificed (a favourite word in the literature) if they enter a well-designed trial in which they will be carefully supervised throughout. The patient, however, may see it differently. It does not even enter her head that she could be sacrificed in the sense of being given an inferior treatment, although this can happen in a bad trial, even today. (See chapter 7 for some current examples and M.H. Pappworth's book *Human Guinea Pigs* for a well-documented and shocking account of some 500 unethical clinical trials in the fifties and sixties.) No, for her the sacrifice lies in agreeing to accept a random allocation of the treatments on offer, having assumed, as all patients naturally do, that her doctor would be giving her personal care based on her unique, personal needs. This is a psychological rather than a physical sacrifice, but no less real for that. The cost of surrendering her will to the impersonal dictate of randomisation should never be under-estimated by researchers who, in their zeal to establish certainty, may be asking for superhuman detachment from patients, and their doctors too.

In truth, of course, most researchers understand full well the distress which may be caused by explaining randomisation and so they will argue that it is more humane to withhold this item of information. Often what they really mean, although few are honest enough to admit it, or at any rate not beyond their closed circle, is that randomisation may be so unpalatable a concept for patients in certain trials that if they are informed about it they will refuse their consent. To buttress their argument for not providing full information in these circumstances, researchers rationalise that so long as the treatments are theoretically equally good – and they will remain so until enough results come in to warrant a firm conclusion one way or the other – the patient is not actually being deprived of any material information.

They themselves do not know all the facts; randomisation is a methodological principle rather than a factual item of knowledge; therefore the patient has no grounds for complaint. But facts are not the sum total of material evidence so far as the patient is concerned. Randomisation is a key feature of the trial; it is therefore a key item of information for the patient. Not to disclose it means that she has not been fully informed about a procedure which she may regard as highly relevant to her decision. This is unethical. Furthermore, it means that her personal preferences have been suborned to the dangerous utilitarian view that a potential social benefit for large numbers of people outweighs the individual's personal values in the here and now. I say 'dangerous' deliberately because any attempt to define 'the greatest good for the greatest number' invariably founders when it comes to quantification. By its very nature anything projected for the future is unknowable whereas we do have a pretty clear idea of what is good in the present and, particularly, what is good for ourselves.

What the patient wants does matter and, ethically, this patient preference should be given equal value with the much-debated treatment preference of doctors. Consider an actual trial now in progress to compare two types of surgical treatment for early breast cancer: simple mastectomy (removal of the whole breast) versus lumpectomy (removal of the tumour only, together with a certain amount of surrounding tissue). Doctors are deeply divided in their opinion as to which method is safest and promises the best outcome for patients. At the present time some doctors are sticking rigidly to mastectomy for all their patients; others are doing lumpectomies equally as a matter of course, but there is no proof that one treatment is better than the other. The mortality figures have shown that mastectomy of any kind does not guarantee that the disease will be eliminated. This is because breast cancer is a systemic disease, which means that by the time the primary tumour manifests itself, the cancer may already have been disseminated into the body and no surgical method is going to cure the cancer. The advantage of a complete mastectomy is that it lessens the chance of the cancer returning to the same site; with lumpectomy there is always the worry that a tiny tumour will escape detection only to reappear later in the same breast, causing considerable distress to the patient.

This trial aims to establish definitive answers to two questions: first, can lumpectomy combined with adjuvant (back-up) radiotherapy reduce local recurrence, and second, is there a significant difference in long-term survival between the two treatments? The underlying question at issue is not cure, but control, and the degree to which it can be achieved. We must be quite clear in our minds about this distinction because it has an important bearing on the patient's choice. If, as the result of the trial, lumpectomy proves to carry no greater risk on either of these scores than mastectomy, then obviously many worried women, and their doctors, will feel reassured about opting for it. Neither treatment promises cure but the less deforming operation does it make it easier to live with the possible continuing presence of cancer. A good result for lumpectomy would also encourage more women in the future to present themselves to their doctors at a time when the lump is still small enough to make the lumpec- tomy operation viable and perhaps curative as well.

This is a very important and well-designed trial, but it is not the first in the field. What distinguishes it from its RCT precedessors is that it is the *first* in this country to advise participating doctors that they should seek informed consent from their patients. Although this requirement is not mandatory, it is clearly stated in the protocol; it has to be considered by every ethical committee to which the protocol is presented, and guidelines have been drawn up to help doctors in their difficult task. It is a small step forward for women, did they but know it, and a giant stride forward for those doctors who are now conscientiously striving to meet this obligation. But is it enough?

Imagine what this tells us about the past, and the present. There are thousands of patients who have been and are being entered into similar trials without knowing that their treatment has been randomly allocated; their doctors will simply have told them that they needed whichever operation had been assigned to them by the computer. Of course, if they had refused the treatment allocated to them they would have been taken out of the trial, but again *without ever knowing* that they had been entered. The majority of those women who did accept the doctor's 'verdict' with a heavy heart were conned, it is no exaggeration to say, into believing that this was a considered, deliberate choice for them. They were not told that there was an alternative; the doctors blatantly deceived them by suggesting that they were getting the 'best' treatment (since this is not known), and they were denied the opportunity to decide for themselves whether they would let the computer do the choosing for them or make up their own minds. They were treated as objects to further the ends of research, but scientific ends, however laudable, can never justify immoral means. An unethical trial procedure invalidates the whole trial.

Deception on this scale has been repeated over and over again in many other clinical trials, but it strikes a particular chill in the context of breast cancer. The reactions of women who know they have this disease vary enormously, depending on their self-image, their personal relationships, their priorities for themselves and their family commitments. Some will want it 'all out' and opt for a mastectomy because they feel that this is the only sure way of eradicating the disease. Others care desperately about losing a breast; they feel that a mastectomy is an assault on their sexuality which threatens everything that makes them feel a woman; they want the least mutilation possible and will beg for a lumpectomy. In between these two viewpoints individual women will take up intermediate positions, balancing risks and benefits according to their own lights and needs. For most women this is going to be the most fearful and distressing experience of their lives. Since there is a legitimate doubt about the respective value of the two treatments, they must be allowed to exercise their right of preference; the alternatives must be presented and they must be asked if they have a preference or whether they will agree to be randomised.

Many doctors, including some of those who do have a preference for one treatment and would therefore not put their patients into a trial, now agree that if a woman has set her heart on a particular treatment, she must be allowed to have it, even if it means she is going against their advice. Doctors who decide not to enter their patients into a trial are, after all, exercising their right to express a treatment preference. Patients have an equal right to express such a preference and it should not be denied to them by entering them into a RCT without informing them about randomisation.

There is an eminent, highly respected breast cancer specialist who has been heard to say about informed consent in RCTs: 'Over my dead body'. Would he say the same if he suspected that *his* body might one day be subjected to a drastic amputation, without his consent, at the whim of a computer? Of course not. It is unthinkable. Moreover, it adds insult to injury to suggest, as does the *Dictionary of Medical Ethics*, (p. 83), that a trial can be ethically justified if the participating doctor would confidently enter a close relative. Most doctors specialising in breast cancer are male; their patients are, with very rare exceptions, female. These doctors may have wives, daughters and sisters. They may admire and cherish the breasts of the women they love, but they do not have breasts of their own. They know the disease and the havoc it wreaks and they desperately want to cure it, but how deeply can they empathise with the anguish it causes? Because they are doctors and see suffering, pain and human misery day after day, even the most compassionate among them have to some extent inured themselves to detachment.

Doctors are as human as the rest of us and in order to get on with their job they do have to protect themselves from being torn apart by their own emotions. The chance to participate in a RCT may seem to offer them an escape route from ineffectual pity, a chance to do something positive. Rightly, they say that they must find better treatments for their patients. Wrongly, they argue that since informing patients of randomised treatment is likely to impose a cruel extra burden on them at a time when they need all their reserves of strength to fight the disease, randomisation should therefore not be disclosed. This argument is wrong because it starts from the wrong premise, namely that randomisation is necessarily the only way to find the answer. If doctors feel that randomisation in a certain trial is unfair to their patients or too difficult to explain, then it is randomisation which has to be abandoned, not the truth. It behoves the researchers to seek an alternative, genuinely humane method of testing the treatment which does not infringe ethical principles. It may take longer, it may not be quite as certain, but it is the only ethical solution. The human mind has never flinched from confronting a challenge and there is no reason to believe that an alternative method of experimentation which is acceptable to patients could not be found, providing there is the will to look for it.

Before we look at some variations on randomisation that have been proposed, it is worth considering what is happening with the current breast cancer trial which advises doctors to seek their patients' informed consent. It appears to be running into problems, which the investigators suspect may be in part due to this requirement, even though it is not obligatory. Too few patients are coming in too slowly. This could be because once patients have been told that there are alternatives – something which they may not have dared to ask for themselves – they then want to make their own choice. This is a speculative guess because there is no mechanism in the trial protocol to pick up the reasons patients are giving for their refusal. What is certain is that some doctors are declining to enter their patients, either because they do not feel able to seek informed consent or because they think that the trial, important though it is, is making an impossible demand on patients by insisting on randomisation. Both these groups are behaving ethically for different reasons. Doctors who honestly feel unable to inform their patients fully but think that it is wrong not to do so should obviously not participate; neither should those doctors who are worried that patients who agree to randomisation may later come to regret bitterly their decision.

There is, however, a third group of doctors participating in this trial who are entering their patients without seeking their informed consent. So long as they have the approval of their ethical committee, they are conforming to the trial protocol and will feel perfectly justified in their conduct for all the reasons we have considered. It would be interesting to know whether these patients form the majority now going through the trial. Again there is no means of gleaning this information from the doctors themselves, for nothing has been written into the protocol to collect data about the way they inform their patients – whether fully or partially.

All is not lost, however. There is a good chance that something useful about informed consent, or the lack of it, will emerge indirectly from a side trial which is being carried out at the same time to compare the degrees of post-operative psychological distress caused by the two treatments. Soon after surgery and again at periods of three and twelve months later, a randomised group of patients is being interviewed in depth by research nurses to ascertain both what they feel about their illness and themselves and what they have been told about the treatment and how the information was conveyed. The dangerous words 'informed consent' will be handled with kid gloves, no doubt, and there is a disturbing ethical ambivalence about making this *post hoc* enquiry after the time when informed consent should have been sought. Randomisation, by contrast, presents no problems in this study because all the patients would have been told at the time of their first questionnaire before treatment that they might be asked to give further interviews which they would be at liberty to refuse.

Despite its blemishes,* this enquiry is a trail-blazing attempt, unique in this country, to discover the real impact of informed consent on

---

* As a member of the working party which has set up this trial I should make it clear that this is a personal view which my colleagues have heard me express but may not share

patients. The only other piece of similar research is, as far as I am aware, being done in Australia where there is an RCT now in progress seeking the same answer. Unfortunately, the Australian trial begs its own question in that it starts by randomising the patients, without their knowledge, into two groups: those in the 'total disclosure' group are being given all the information possible and then treated according to whether they consent to be randomised or express a preference; the other 'standard practice' group are not being asked to give informed consent. The aim, of course, is to get hard data on patient's reactions to informed consent: Do they really want it? Does it make them feel better or worse after the event? Are the uninformed patients eventually going to be more or less distressed? Valuable and necessary information, certainly, but there is a strong whiff of Alice in Wonderland logic about the notion that you can subject an ethical principle to scientific testing. Either a moral right exists, or it does not. If it does, then it is universal and no one has the right to deny it to anyone. In this trial, the patients who have been randomised into the 'standard practice' group are being denied that right. As we shall see in Part Three, there are other ethical ways of determining what individual patients feel about giving their informed consent and, much more important, of ensuring that each individual patient gets what she needs.

VARIATIONS ON RANDOMISATION

The model of randomisation described in the Australian trial was devised by an American biostatistician, Dr Marvin Zelen, specifically to deal with the practical and ethical difficulties that doctors encounter in explaining the principle.* Thus, in a straightforward cancer trial comparing two treatments, all the patients are first randomised, without their knowledge, into either a control group in which they will receive the best standard therapy or an experimental group in which they are fully informed about the trial and their consent is sought. The obvious advantage of this model is that at least those patients who have been randomised to the new treatment now know that they are in a trial and have the option to accept or refuse the treatment. The

---

* 'A New Design for Randomized Clinical Trials', *New England Journal of Medicine*, 1979, 300; 22: 1242-45

disadvantage is equally obvious. The patients in the control 'do not seek consent' group have been randomised without their knowledge; they have not been told that they are in a trial and they, therefore, have no options.

Attractive though this model appears to many researchers, ethically it remains an unsatisfactory compromise. Zelen is at pains to answer the three possible ethical objections which he thinks could be raised. First, he argues that there is nothing wrong in withholding information from the control group about the trial because these patients are getting what they naturally assume they will receive – the best standard therapy.

He phrases the second objection somewhat disingenuously. Instead of asking the real question, whether it is ethical not to inform all patients that they may have the chance of getting the experimental treatment, he twists it into the following form: 'Is it ethical not to offer the experimental treatment to all patients?' But this is never a possibility in an RCT, the fundamental purpose of which is to compare and measure treatments. By its very nature, it is never going to offer the experimental treatment to *everyone* but merely the opportunity through randomisation. On the Zelen model, all the doctors know that every eligible patient has this opportunity but none of the patients does, whichever group she has been assigned. This fact is a fatal flaw in the ethical construct of the scheme and no amount of rationalisation can redeem it. For instance, to say that some patients will have 'the privilege of receiving an experimental treatment', or that those in the control group will be far better managed than if they were not in the trial, may reassure doctors, but it is of no value as far as the patients are concerned because they are in a state of ignorance.

Zelen's final concern is whether patients should be told that data about their treatment will be used, and for what purpose. He resolves it to his own satisfaction by pointing out that so long as patients are not put at risk by being identified there is no need to reveal these details to them. He states, quite correctly, that this is being done all the time, as for instance when diseases are notified anonymously to central registries. Again this plausible justification slides over the real question which should be asked about RCTs. It is not a question of whether this non-disclosure would threaten the patient's right to confidentiality (a whole other ball game in medical ethics), but, what and how much should all trial patients be told about their participation?

Obviously, to tell the patients in the control group that their treatment progress will be compared with another treatment could alert them to the fact that they are in a trial.

The Zelen proposal for dealing with randomisation does not stand up ethically. Is there any other way of getting round the problem of explaining randomisation to patients? And if not, must the principle be rejected, at least for certain trials? 'No' to the first question will mean 'yes' to the second. Zelen himself has now come up with an alternative suggestion which is enticingly simple and appears to be totally ethical. It proposes that patients should be randomised first and told afterwards. They will then be fully informed about the trial and their consent sought.*

Morally, there is nothing questionable about the order of procedure because randomising is not, strictly speaking, part of the treatment; it is merely a method of apportionment. Nothing physical has been done to the patient without her consent. However, if we carefully think through its implementation, the alarm bells begin to ring. For example, an over-enthusiastic doctor could be tempted to paint a glowing picture of the benefits of the trial to the patient and, in particular, of the treatment that had been allotted to her. It is no denigration of patients to point out that they are especially vulnerable to suggestion in these circumstances and could easily be persuaded that it would be churlish, if not downright foolish, to refuse this privileged opportunity. Patients might be subtly influenced to believe that once randomised they are in the trial and there is no going back. As Beecher has written, and as many doctors know full well from their own experience, 'patients will, if they trust their doctor, accede to almost any request he cares to make'.† So, although this method of explaining randomisation is, in theory, perfectly ethical, it does present problems in practice.

What about a trial where randomisation is used on a group basis rather than individually? For example, the DHSS is currently running a long-term study to see whether there are advantages in screening for breast cancer by regular clinical and mammographic examination (X ray of the breasts) as compared with regular breast self-examination. Four population centres have been selected – two for each

---

*   'Innovations in the Designs of Clinical Trials in Breast Cancer', *Breast Cancer Research and Treatment*, 1983, 3; 137–142
†   'Consent in Clinical Experimentation: Myth and Reality', *Journal of the American Medical Association*, 1966, 195: 1; 34

method, and each adopting slight variations which are also being closely compared. Four further centres have been selected as control groups and in these areas no form of screening is being offered. Here the equivalent groups of women, defined by age, are simply being monitored to see whether there is a significant difference in the number of cases of breast cancer being picked up as a result of screening. Although there has been selection in the sense that the eight centres have been chosen and have agreed to participate in the trial according to the terms of the protocol, as far as the women themselves are concerned it is a matter of pure random chance into which group they fall. The women who live in the screening areas are invited to participate and can accept or refuse as they wish; those in the control groups have no idea that they are, in a negative sense, also participating in the trial. Nothing vital is being withheld from these latter groups because although trials in America, Holland and Sweden have shown some promising results for breast cancer screening, there is nothing conclusive to indicate that it could be a significant life-saving measure. Unfortunately, even early detection in breast cancer does not guarantee cure, so it may ultimately prove to be more ethical as well as sounder medical practice to concentrate medical resources on improving methods of treatment which will benefit many more women than the small numbers picked up by unselective screening. (Symptomatic or high-risk women already have screening facilities available to them.)

These are the questions the DHSS trial is seeking to resolve. The problem is how to present them to the general public without exciting a wholesale demand for screening which cannot be met. The control groups who are unaware that they are participating in the trial are not at this stage being denied a proven benefit; on the other hand, do they have a right to know about their negative involvement? If they do, it could mean that they too will insist on the screening measures now being offered to the experimental groups and thus torpedo the trial before it has had a chance to come up with results. A further problem raised by this kind of community-based trial is that in order to avoid 'contaminating' the outcome, the control groups may be denied certain basic health education information. For example, in a trial testing a new treatment for hypertension is it ethical to withhold from the control group proven facts such as the desirability of reducing salt intake? There are no easy answers to these questions but we, as well as the doctors, should be asking them and jointly debating their solution

ALTERNATIVES TO RANDOMISATION

Randomisation *per se* is neither ethical nor unethical; it is simply a neutral instrument of scientific measurement. If it is properly used (in both the ethical and medical senses of 'proper') by the doctors who apply it, and is properly (in the sense of adequately) understood by the patients to whom it is applied, then it does provide a real ethical as well as scientific benefit in that it ensures, first, that the trial will be run impartially without favouring one group of patients at the expense of another, and second, that doctors are not inflicting unproven, possibly harmful treatments on their patients. However, if for any of the reasons I have outlined in this chapter, randomisation in a trial is not always acceptable either to patients, or doctors, or both, what alternatives are available to them?

The 'randomisers' emphatically deny that there is any such thing as a valid alternative. They discredit those that have been tried for varying reasons: too anecdotal (a very dirty word in these circles) to be taken seriously; 'mostly traditional and time-dishonoured',* or else so weak and unreliable as to be almost useless. They also sometimes charge with hypocrisy those doctors who hold off entering their patients into RCTs for their own 'ethical' reasons but who nonetheless eagerly scan the journals for the published results of their colleagues' research. However, to be fair to these and other conscientious doctors, what else can they do? Either they continue with procedures they learnt as medical students or they endeavour to keep up with developments, and that includes following the progress of RCTs since they are generally acknowledged to be the best way of ascertaining the benefits of a new treatment. The best of these trials are, as we have seen, run according to rigorous scientific method; they usually have the backing of well-respected academic departments whose pronouncements are important and cannot be ignored. Those who run the trials feel their responsibility keenly and are strongly motivated by the laudable desire to inject some science into medicine. What they are not so willing to accept is that (as we saw in chapter 5) RCTs are limited in their

* David H. Spodick, 'The Randomized Controlled Clinical Trial: Scientific and Ethical Bases', *American Journal of Medicine*, 1982, 73: 420-45

scope, both in the questions they can ask and the extrapolations that researchers can legitimately make from the evidence. However water-tight it may seem, and however carefully it has been interpreted and pre-sented by the investigators, in the final analysis the evidence from an RCT is no more immune from wishful thinking and personal prejudice than evidence derived from other sources. An editorial in *World Medicine* (21 March 1984) pounced gleefully on this quandary when it pointed out that in the same week separate articles in the *British Medical Journal* and the *Lancet* had come out with flatly contradictory conclusions about a straightforward report of recent American research into the relationship between blood cholesterol and heart disease. 'One sus-pects,' it chortled, 'that the root of this schism between the evangelical interventionists and the conservative "abominable no-men", who are accused by their adversaries of nihilism, lies more in differences of personality than in science.' My point precisely.

It would be tedious and unprofitable here to consider most of the alternatives to RCTs in any detail except for one that does appeal to many doctors who are keen to pursue useful research if they can do so without compromising themselves or their patients. This is the system of a concurrent control series by which patients, carefully matched for certain characteristics, are then allocated comparative treatments according to their preference, or the doctor's, as they decide. The objection from the randomisers to this type of trial is predictable: it has no built-in safeguard against doctors making a biased selection of their patients; nor, in the case, for example, of a multi-centre trial in which the treatments combine surgery with radiotherapy, is there any mechanism to nullify the variables introduced by different treatment techniques and follow-up. Imperfect this kind of trial may be – like all human endeavour – but it probably has more merit, scientifically speaking, than those who advocate randomisation-at-all-costs are pre-pared to concede. Such trials are ethically acceptable to both patients and doctors, and the researchers who favour them are well aware of the methodological hazards and do their utmost to counter them.

ARE PLACEBOS ETHICAL?

The placebo has been defined as 'any therapy (or component of therapy) that is deliberately or knowingly used for its nonspecific, psy-chologic or psycho-physiologic effect, or that ... unknown to the patient or therapist, is without specific activity for the condition being treated.'* It has a long history in medical practice and doctors resort to it either because they do not have anything better to offer or to appease patients who insist they must have something. Doctors are inclined to blame their patients for having unrealistic expectations of cure, and although this is very often true we might reasonably ask who has encouraged these expectations, if not doctors? Most placebos are inert, that is to say they have no active pharmacological properties, but their effects can be as positive as any real drug. Beecher points out that placebos are 'powerful therapeutic tools, having one-half to two-thirds as much power to relieve pain of pathologic origin as the optimal dose of morphine given at the rate of 10 mg per 70 kg body weight.'† It is not just 'the mixture' or the little pink pills which work as placebos. Bok maintains that any medical procedure including 'X rays, vitamin preparations, antibiotics and even surgery can function as placebos' whenever they do not have a specific effect on the condition for which they are prescribed.

Essentially a placebo works by deception. The patient imagines she is receiving a specific treatment for her condition; however, the relief she experiences may by physiologically real. Doctors generally have not been overly perturbed by the lies they tell when prescribing a placebo, arguing that if the remedy works then they have benefited their patient and no harm done. Ethically, a question mark hangs over the use of placebos. Do doctors resort to them too easily instead of asking themselves whether it would not be wiser to spend more time explaining to patients that medication for every ill is not always possible and suggesting ways in which they can help themselves? Moreover, it is not even medically true that placebos are harmless if not always beneficial; this has been amply substantiated by Bok who cites several cases in which placebos have induced extremely unpleasant side effects and even a drug-like dependency.

Placebos are frequently used in drug trials as an alternative to the experimental drug and, almost without exception, it is a condition of the trial protocol that patients should not be informed that that is what they may be getting instead of a specific treatment. The investigators justify this deception on the grounds that they cannot get a fair

* Arthur K. Shapiro quoted by Sissela Bok in 'The Ethics of Giving Placebos', *Scientific American*, 1974, 231; 5: 17-23
† *Research and the Individual: Human Studies*, p. 76

comparison between the two 'treatments' if patients are going to suspect that theirs might be the placebo. Furthermore, to give them this information might destroy the trial because a lot of patients would refuse their consent. In a double blind trial, the participating doctors do usually know that a placebo is one of the options, but they do not know which patient is getting what.

There are several problems about this practice. The first is that the patient is being denied her right to act as an autonomous, self-determining person. Decisions are being made for her, maybe 'for her own good', maybe not. Take the flagrantly unethical case of the women in San Antonio, Texas, who in 1971 went to their family planning clinics for the Pill and were given a dummy instead. They were told that some (unspecified) research was being carried out, but neither they *nor* the clinic doctors knew that the women were in a trial to test the side effects of the Pill and that some of them would be getting a placebo instead. The researchers were able to prove that the placebo group experienced many of the same side effects as women on the Pill – big deal! – and seven of the women in the placebo group (10 per cent) suffered the worst side effect of all – an unwanted pregnancy. All the compensation they got for this gross fraud was an expression of regret from Dr Goldzeiher, the leader of the trial, that he could not arrange for abortions as this was against the state law.

The second straight moral problem is that doctors who put their patients into trials and do not tell them that they may be getting a placebo are seriously abusing their patients' trust in them. The patient has come for treatment to benefit her, not to offer herself for research to benefit others. If the doctor thinks it is necessary to enter her into a trial then she must be told, and if one of the alternatives is a placebo, then she should know that as well. Interestingly, although there is a great deal of speculation about the distorting effects that such knowledge would have on the trial, no research has been done to ascertain the reality. Is there any reason to suppose that if patients are informed, exactly as their doctors are, that they are taking part in a double blind trial in which they might get a placebo, the effect of knowing this will be any more detrimental to the outcome of the trial than the doctor's knowledge? It could be argued that by equalising the variables in this way the trial is sounder in its concept.

Of course, it all depends on the nature of the experimental

92   *Whose body is it?*

treatment. If it is for something comparatively mild, say a new drug for a chronic but not life-threatening condition, patients would probably quite readily accept the chance to be involved in the experiment, as long as they were assured that if they did need real treatment at any stage they would be taken off the placebo. But what if the experimental treatment promises a crucial benefit to the patient which, if she knew about it, she would not want to forgo?

Take the recent example of the spina bifida trial which some doctors were moved to publicise because they thought it was too outrageous to be allowed. This is an MRC trial involving 3,000 women in twenty centres, all of whom have already had a spina bifida child and therefore run a 20 to 1 risk of producing another child with a similar defect. Studies have already shown that a vitamin supplement called Pregnavite Forte F, which includes vitamin B and folic acid, appears to reduce the incidence of spina bifida. Not satisfied with these very encouraging but statistically unvalidated results, the researchers want to establish precisely the protective effects of each ingredient and make sure that there are not other undesirable side effects, although these are hardly likely with vitamins. The trial randomly allocates the women to four groups: 25 per cent receiving Pregnavite Forte F in its entirety, 25 per cent getting vitamin B on its own, 25 per cent getting only the folic acid, and 25 per cent getting a placebo. This means that 750 women are completely unprotected and another 1,500 are at risk because they are getting only half the treatment.

What woman, offered an uncertain but good chance to save her baby from an uncertain but appalling fate, would agree to enter such a trial if she knew the conditions? What does she care about statistical significance, and why should she care? In the name of what implacable stony-faced god of numbers is she being asked to sacrifice her child? And it is, after all, quite usual for doctors to use drugs without completely understanding how they work. This is an example of statistics being used to produce inadmissible evidence – every deformed child born to a woman in the unprotected group would count as such – and it is a fair bet that any researcher who knew his own wife to be at risk would not want her to enter the trial. In such circumstances, there is only one ethical, humane way to gather the evidence and that is by continuing to analyse the data as they come in. As Professor John Corber, a pediatrician who is strongly opposed to the trial, wrote in a letter to the *Guardian* (20 May 1983), 'if women ask for and receive the readily available Pregnavite Forte F, then one will never know (*and it doesn't matter*) which women might have had a baby with a neural tube defect had they not taken this protection.' (my emphasis)

Patients who unwittingly receive placebos in trials are being manipulated and treated with a good deal less dignity and respect than they deserve. Doctors who subscribe to this kind of deception are demeaning themselves and threatening the integrity of their profession, because the more often this kind of behaviour is exposed the more suspicious and antagonistic the public will become. And that is counter-productive for all concerned.

WHEN TO STOP AND OTHER PROBLEMS FOR DOCTORS

It is commonly stipulated that doctors who enter their patients into a trial must not have a preference for one of the treatments because it would be unethical to expose their patients to the risk of getting what they consider to be an inferior treatment. Admirable though this counsel may be, how often is it put into practice? Most experienced doctors cannot help feeling intuitively that one treatment is preferable, even if they accept intellectually that if it is not proven it should be tested. By the very fact of joining the trial doctors agree to suspend their own clinical judgement and to rely on the opinion of independent observers. Although a double blind trial may seem to make this easier for them, it can in practice prove more difficult, because they feel that they are working in the dark and possibly against their instincts.

Moreover, what should they do if, as the results start to come in, it appears that their preference is confirmed or, alternatively, that the other treatment is superior? The trial has targeted a specific total of patients to avoid the danger of making a hasty judgement based on insufficient evidence, and it is important to see it through to the end to make sure that the emerging trend is properly tested for its significance. If too many patients are withdrawn early, this conclusion is postponed and it complicates the task of assessing the results. Although doctors and patients both are supposed to be free to withdraw as and when they wish, in reality the subtle pressures imposed on doctors not to let the trial down can be hard to resist.

No amount of ingenious statistical checks and external reviews can really resolve this moral dilemma for the sensitive doctor who may feel intolerably oppressed by conflicting obligations. Does the doctor give priority to an individual ethic or a collective ethic? Is the doctor primarily a researcher or a clinician? On the one hand there is the patient who has trustingly placed herself in the doctor's care; on the other, there is the doctor's obligation to conform to the trial requirements and pay regard to the wider benefits it may bring to a large group of future patients. Which matters more? These problems will be examined more closely in Part Three. Meanwhile, this comment from a critic of the blanket use of randomised trials for everything seems apposite: 'If morality and methodology conflict, it seems to us that the onus is upon us to develop methodologies that harmonise with our morality, rather than compromise with morality on the probably false assumption that we are dealing with an immaculate methodology.'*

The whole mechanism of an RCT is geared to the efficient, impartial collection of statistically valid information, but implementing it can sometimes be alienating and dehumanising. RCTs can induce a dangerous mood of hubris in those who champion them and tempt them to overlook the fact that even the best designed RCT is never going to be impeccable in its execution. Although most of the current alternatives are inadequate, and none can provide the same degree of certainty as a first-class RCT, we must remind the RCT's supporters that the uncertain goal of 'certainty' can sometimes be too high a price to pay in humanitarian and ethical terms. Furthermore, as we shall see in the next chapter, there are still far too many slipshod, ill-conceived and highly unethical trials which are masquerading as respectable RCTs and managing to slip through the net of ethical committees and other review bodies for anyone to feel comfortably complacent about the present situation.

*   John Heron, *Draft Policy Statement on the Use of the Randomised Trial*, Research Council for Complementary Medicine

7 In whose hands?

> Unless we have someone or something we can respect,
> a humility before something or someone greater than
> ourselves, to stimulate and protect our idealism, we
> shall fall prey to self-interest again and again. In the face
> of determined self-interest, without any yardstick to
> check us, no Hippocratic Oath, no Declaration of
> Geneva and no ethical guidelines will ever have the
> slightest influence in moulding our actions.
>
> Brian P. Bliss and Alan G. Johnson
> *Aims and Motives in Clinical Medicine*

'Outrage! Scandal!' scream the advertisements put out by the animal liberation organisations which want to see an end to all experimentation on animals. They describe in lurid detail examples of experiments they deem to be cruel and unnecessary and they are able to quote precise figures for the experiments performed each year because, by law, every animal experiment has to be approved and licensed by the Home Office. Lengthy forms have to be filled in, justifying the experiments and explaining the process, and the rules for their proper conduct are posted up in all laboratories using animals.

No one knows how many human beings in this country are annually involved in experimentation, whether it be non-therapeutic or applied clinical research using patients. There is no equivalent government department issuing forms and demanding that certain rules be followed for the conduct of clinical trials. There is no central registry recording the number and type of clinical trials in progress. There is no law requiring that every proposal for a trial be notified to a research ethical committee or similar review body, and there is no system for monitoring even those trials that have been approved by such a body. No one even knows how many research ethical committees there are, or how they run themselves, because there are no statutory regulations for their conduct. Ethical committees came into existence less than twenty years ago and they are still lacking in several areas in Britain.

That ethical committees exist at all is due in great measure to the shocking disclosures, by Maurice Pappworth in this country and the late Henry Beecher in America, of grossly immoral trials.* Both respected doctors, they blew the whistle on their erring colleagues in the sixties – twenty years, be it noted, after the Nuremberg revelations – and for his pains Pappworth, at least, is commonly alluded to as 'over-emotional' and 'hysterical'. The Royal College of Physicians hurriedly established a working party in 1967 to examine the situation and it takes the credit for urging that ethical committees be set up and for issuing some guidelines for their structure. Since then, successive governments have been satisfied to leave it to the medical profession to regulate itself without further enquiry or supervision. Both the DHSS and the BMA periodically remind doctors of their duties in respect of research, but there is no system of follow-up.

Which is the greater scandal? Undoubtedly animals are suffering and being sacrificed needlessly, and the 1876 Cruelty to Animals Act does need revision, but at least animals have the law on their side and there is currently a Home Office working party considering ways of tightening it up. Human beings have no such protection. Patients and volunteers are entirely dependent on the good faith and self-imposed restraints of the medical profession. How certain can we be that doctors and researchers will always put the patients' interests before their own and observe the high ethical standards of the Declaration of Helsinki? The brutal answer is that we have no guarantee whatsoever. We can only hope and trust.

WHO DECIDES?

When in 1973, at the request of the Chief Medical Officer, the Royal College of Physicians issued a further report on the scope and structure of ethical committees, it emphasised that the aim of these bodies was to safeguard patients, healthy volunteers and the reputation of the profession. It recommended that the committees

* See select bibliography and chapter references

should be kept small and constituted in such a way as not to hinder unreasonably the advancement of medical knowledge. It also suggested that a lay member should be included on the committee and that the medical members should be experienced clinical researchers. By 1980, the BMA realised with some embarrassment that although it had stated in its *Handbook of Medical Ethics* that research proposals should always be referred to 'a properly constituted' ethical committee, no one had the faintest idea what this meant. In all those reports and committee deliberations, no one had thought to draw up some criteria. Hastily, the BMA wrote to all ninety-eight medical officers in England and Wales asking them to describe the function of their committees. Twenty-five did not respond, and from the answers of the others the BMA was forced to conclude that 'the results are so variable that no given constitution of membership of an ethical committee for clinical research predominates'.* Lay members were included on only two-thirds of the committees and GPs were even more sparsely represented.

The terse style of this report disguises the serious concern felt by the BMA. What it had discovered was a totally lamentable state of affairs: local committees, haphazardly appointed and with no clear idea of their remit, were acting without proper terms of reference and with no system of accountability. Three years later the BMA's Central Ethical Committee has come up with some proposals 'to take the whole thing in hand', as its present chairman, Dr Macara, puts it, the main one being a National Committee to act as a central co-ordinating body for local ethical committees. Before it can be set on the road, however, its terms of reference, its functions, its funding and the selection criteria for membership have yet to be resolved, and this will entail interminable further discussions among all the interested bodies – the Royal Colleges, the teaching faculties, the MRC, the GMC, the DHSS and so on. Each of these institutions is obsessively jealous of its privileges and powers, and will be reluctant to cede an iota. They may not even be willing to allow the BMA its claim to act as supremo. So, while the political wrangling goes on, local committees will continue to bumble along, some reasonably conscientiously no doubt, but many more, I fear, functioning no better than the committee of this Central London hospital whose practices were described to me by a lay member.

* 'Local Ethical Committees', *British Medical Journal*, 1981, 282: 1010

In the seven years that she has been on the committee, she can recall meeting only three times with the other members to discuss changes of principle. The rest of the time the committee's work is done by correspondence. On average, three research applications a month are sent out to the members for their comments, and if they do not answer after one reminder from the secretary their silence is taken to mean approval. She is fairly confident that all the research projects within the hospital have been submitted to the committee but admits there is no system for checking up, nor of monitoring the research in progress. Her committee considers that informed consent is of prime importance and should always be sought, but again it has no means of finding out whether it is done, how and by whom. The consent form I saw was typical of its kind, an off-putting document consisting of a series of didactic statements expressed in language which made no concessions to the average patient's lack of medical knowledge. It was, furthermore, deceptive for it described only the new treatment under trial – a drug for male patients with prostatic carcinoma – and was to be presented only to those patients who had already been randomised for this treatment. The alternative standard treatment for this disease at this stage is an orchidectomy, (surgical removal of the testes). The investigators had stated in the protocol that prior randomisation was necessary, to which the committee agreed, on the grounds that given the choice, few patients would opt for castration and this would bias the trial!

Well, naturally, it would, but once again we have to ask whose interests the investigators are serving? Men suffering from this disease are in the same situation as women with breast cancer, or conceivably even worse. Surgery may well make them impotent; the drug may have the same effect (a fact, incidentally not clearly spelled out in the consent form). Given the seriousness of their condition, it is both heartless in the extreme and totally unethical not to allow them to know what the alternatives are and to spell out their implications. Of course it is necessary to test the new treatment thoroughly, but when there is a conflict of this order between the patient's preference and the rigorous demands of an RCT, there can surely be no question about which takes priority.

Patients must be allowed to select themselves for treatment, having made their own calculations about the respective risks and benefits, and having decided for themselves what matters most for them. It is their values which count and must be respected, not the interests of science or, more dangerously, the personal interests of the investigators. Too bad if this means that the investigators will have to wait longer before they can give a firm opinion. Better that than to plumb the depths of callous cynicism evinced by the attitude that what the mind does not know the heart cannot grieve over. The patient's personal welfare must always be put before the interests of scientific enquiry.

It is supremely ironical that some of the doctors who make such a fuss about the purity of the randomising principle are prepared to be so very careless about the purity of ethical principles. Inhuman research is inexcusable and quite unacceptable. The right and only answer to the perfectly proper medical quest for advance is 'Humane research, not no research', and ethical committees could do no better than to adopt this as a guiding principle for their decisions.*

The literature shows that there are some ethical committees in Britain which do recognise that their prime responsibility is towards patients, and these are constantly seeking to improve their methods. But, alas, they are the rare exception. Too many ethical committees are secretive about their practices, confused about their criteria and far too biased towards research interests in their membership. Few, for example, are known to have made a positive move to widen their representation by inviting junior hospital doctors, GPs, nurses, community medicine practitioners and at least one lay member, along the lines suggested by the BMA in its proposal for a model constitution. They resist external regulation and supervision, regarding this as unwarranted interference. The worst of them are élitist and unaccountable, and their very existence may be more of a threat than a benefit to patients because they can provide the perfect cover for unscrupulous research. 'The ethical committee has approved our research, so it must be all right' is a dubious justification if the approval has been based not on established criteria but on subjective opinion. Pappworth and Vernon Coleman (also a doctor) have pointed out how easy it is for the medical members of an ethical committee to be swayed in their judgement by quite extraneous factors like their friendship for colleagues, their personal ambition and their career interests. †

Worse, perhaps, than all this is the fact that so many ethical

---

* R.A. McCance quoted by Beecher from *The Practice of Experimental Medicine*, Proceedings of the Royal Society of Medicine, 1951, 44: 189–94 (but not found by the author)

† See select bibliography and chapter references

committees are dreadfully inefficient. Heaven knows what happens in areas where there is no committee at all, but even when there is one its existence is no guarantee that doctors will submit their projects to it for approval. On 6 November 1983, *Observer* journalist Mike Durham reported a trial that had been going on with pregnant Asian women in a hospital under the Brent Health Authority for nearly five months without the knowledge of the district ethical committee and, needless to say, without the consent of the women. Asians living in Britain are known to be prone to vitamin D deficiency. The aim of the trial, conceived by a registrar in obstetrics, was to see whether 'calcium supplementation is of value and effect on fetal growth'. Calcium deficiency in adults is known as calcium osteomalacia, and it is thought by many doctors that if it is passed on in pregnancy to the foetus it may cause serious later complications including fits, brain damage and even death. The women were randomised into three groups, two receiving a different combined dose of calcium and vitamin D daily, and the control group receiving nothing at all. Junior doctors, some of whom were participating reluctantly in the research, became increasingly uneasy about it, especially as they suspected that there were women in the trial who were already at risk because of calcium deficiency. They reported it to a senior consultant who asked the ethical committee to investigate. Although the committee ordered the trial to be suspended immediately while it made enquiries, in fact it continued for another five weeks, apparently because of a 'misunderstanding', which says nothing at all for the committee's authority.

For every bad trial that hits the headlines, one wonders how many more shamble through, putting patients at risk, compromising unwilling juniors and other members of the health team who fear for their promotion prospects if they express dissent and even getting published in journals whose editors do not bother to check out the terms of reference. If bad design and poor execution were not hazard enough, there are also far too many cases of downright fraud as Terry Hamblin, a consultant haematologist, reported with jokey ferocity in *World Medicine* (21 March 1984) 'If fame is the spur, then it takes guts to be honest.'

Obviously, most doctors and researchers do their best to behave ethically, but can it really be right that those in whose hands we place our trust, our hope and our lives can be left entirely to themselves to make the rules and play the game? The answer is surely no, but if the

medical profession wants to protect itself from over-zealous bureau-
crats and legal sanctions, then it is going to have to open its doors to the
outside world and prepare itself to be both more candid about its
problems and more receptive to informed criticism.

WHO PAYS?

Although it is the research ethical committee which acts as final
arbitrator of a research proposal, if the project involves money (and
most do) then it will first have been submitted to the organisation
which is funding the research. Approximately £100 million per year is
spent on medical research, and it is apportioned thus from the
following sources:

Medical Research Council	21%
Health departments	4%
Private charities	11%
Pharmaceutical industry	64%

Further government funds come from the University Grants Committee to support university medical departments.*

The figures speak louder than any words. One of the wealthiest
industries in the country, which reaps profits in the region of £250 to
£300 million annually from the National Health Service, is also the
chief paymaster, by a huge margin, of medical research. One-third of
the pharmaceutical industry's research and development budget is
spent on looking for new drugs, another third on clinical trials and the
remainder on producing and marketing its products. Although drug
companies usually have a vast battery of products on offer, the major
proportion of their profits will come from one or two 'wonder drugs'
which have become essential treatment for some diseases. It would be
foolish to deny that the introduction of many such drugs in the last forty
years has brought great benefits. Lives have been saved and many formerly intractable diseases have been brought under control. They
have also brought many problems in their wake.

Despite the extensive toxicity testing drugs undergo before being
licensed for sale, dire side effects may still emerge later. It is estimated
that iatrogenic disease (illness caused by the treatment) is suffered

* Figures obtained from *Dictionary of Medical Ethics*, 'Research Funding', p. 374

by 10 per cent of all patients, and most of that is the result of drugs. Even more alarming, many drugs which are used for preventative purposes or to alleviate disorders that would eventually get better on their own, may kill or seriously disable one in 10,000 patients. Because the rewards are so high, particularly in the field of chronic conditions like arthritis, high blood pressure and so on, the companies are eager to jump on the bandwagon and so there is a proliferation of what are called the 'me-too' drugs, each promising a special benefit and, unfortunately, too often producing a special and most undesirable side effect.

There has been plenty of recent media coverage of some of the highly questionable practices indulged in by the drug companies to recruit their doctor-investigators. It is now well known that GPs, who are the main collaborators in these trials, are encouraged to participate with the lure of lavish all-expenses-paid trips to exotic pleasure spots and handsome presents. It is perhaps less well known that the companies pay GPs a fee for their services and that although they can submit the project to an ethical committee if they wish, there is no obligation to do so because it has been agreed 'that clinical trials in general practice should not be *obstructed by administrative difficulties* in obtaining ethical clearance' (my emphasis). This statement comes in the foreword to the code of practice 'for the clinical assessment of licensed medicinal products in general practice' which has been drawn up jointly by the BMA, the Royal College of General Practitioners (RCGP) and the Association of the British Pharmaceutical Industry (ABPI).*

The code itself is comprehensive and uncompromising. If doctors follow its guidelines conscientiously and conform to the Declaration of Helsinki as they are recommended, patients should have no fears. But that is a big 'if'. GPs, as we are frequently reminded, are harassed and over-extended. They may 'forget' to tell their patients that the drug they are offering is in a trial; they may tell the patients how to take the drug but they have no way of knowing whether the patients follow their instructions; they may not pay sufficient attention to the patients' complaints of side effects, and they may not report them as they should on the yellow cards which are provided for this purpose. Enough of these omissions on a large scale and the trial becomes worthless, possibly dangerous.

* *British Medical Journal*, 1983, 286: 1295-97

The Committee on the Safety of Medicines was set up after the Thalidomide disaster to control and monitor the use and effects of licensed drugs, but recent revelations about highly unsatisfactory drugs for arthritis like Osmosin and Opren have shown that it is a sleepy and inefficient body which relies far too uncritically for its information on doctors and drug companies and does not exert any real control over the way the drugs are marketed. There is no lay representative on the committee and it refuses either to accept complaints from patients or to release any information it may have gathered about side effects to the lay population. Time after time it has been unforgivably slow in alerting doctors about those hazards it has discovered. In every way it seems to be more concerned to act as a guard dog for medical and commercial interests than as the watch dog it should be for the public's safety.

A new pressure group called Drug Watch is determined to force reform on the CSM. We need a similar lay initiative to ensure that the research which doctors undertake, whether funded by the drug companies, the research charities or the government, is always necessary and beneficial. Vernon Coleman estimates that at least 20 per cent of research is sheer duplication and that too much of it is directed towards 'glamorous' projects which attract money and prestige rather than towards worthier but less rewarding areas.* When the BMA, or any other organisation, gets down to the nitty gritty of standardising the structure and functions of the ethical committees, we must make sure that our voice is heard and heeded. This is not to impugn the integrity of the medical profession which, in the main, is concerned to carry out research ethically. Self-regulation by a powerful group, however carefully administered, is simply not adequate to ensure the security of patients and volunteers, especially those who may fall into the hands of researchers who are over-enthusiastic or negligent. If we want the benefits that medical research can bring us, then we must also be involved in the task of deciding how they are to be achieved without sacrificing those people who lend their bodies to the cause of science on our behalf, irrespective of whether they achieve some benefit themselves.

---

* Vernon Coleman, *The Paper Doctors*, M. Temple-Smith, 1977

SPECIAL CASES AND HEALTHY VOLUNTEERS

Children are probably the best-protected patients of all today. As Beecher and Pappworth have shown, this has not always been the case, particularly in America, but in this country the law has proved a strong safeguard, just because it is so unclear as to what is permissible, especially in non-therapeutic research, on minors. Even when parents have been willing to give their informed consent, doctors have been reluctant to take any chances for fear of later prosecution were anything to go seriously wrong. The result has been that many minimally invasive procedures which would be perfectly acceptable to adult patients have not been done on children.

The British Pediatric Association has produced detailed guidelines to aid ethical committees considering research applications, particularly those which are non-therapeutic, or not of direct benefit to the child patient.* The risk/benefit principle has been carefully defined and every possible eventuality considered. Basically, only procedures carrying a very small risk are allowed in non-therapeutic research, and in cases where the research is intended to benefit the participating children, the ethical committee has to be completely satisfied, first, that it really is necessary and second, that it will be conducted with the utmost care and caution.

We ought to be much more concerned about elderly patients, both inside and outside hospital. Frequently they are confused about what they have agreed to and many health professionals feel that they are inadequately supervised, particularly if they are in a trial as out-patients or under their GP. Some worry about the validity of much of the research that is being done on the elderly, and others question whether they should be involved at all. This is a growing category of patients whose needs deserve much more attention.

The mentally handicapped and the mentally ill, including those who have been involuntarily admitted to hospital, also need special protection. As we saw in chapter 3, this latter group is particularly vulnerable because it can be too easily assumed that their refusal to consent to treatment is irrational and that it is therefore permissible to overrule them. Furthermore, the consent obtained from relatives may not always be given in the best of faith if they are hostile or indifferent to the patient.

* *British Medical Journal,* 1980, 1:229–31

Finally, there are the healthy volunteers who offer their bodies for non-therapeutic research. Animal studies are frequently insufficient for evaluating drugs in their early stages, and so there is an increasing need to find volunteers who will agree to act as human guinea pigs before the drugs are submitted to clinical studies with patients. About 10,000 people a year volunteer themselves in this way; they may be doctors, medical students, hospital workers, laboratory technicians and people working in the pharmaceutical industry, or they may be drawn from the armed forces or the general public. Although these people appear to be in a better position than patients to give their free informed consent, there are reasons to be concerned about the terms of their participation.

Two recent cases spotlight the problems. The first was the revelation early in 1984 that a commercial organisation, the Charterhouse Research Unit, had enlisted students and young unemployed people to test a new cancer drug believed to inhibit tumour growth, for which they were being paid £250 a month. The trial was disturbing on several counts: it had not been submitted to an ethical committee for approval; the financial payment was much higher than is normally considered proper; there were serious worries that the drug might produce certain rare cancers; the participants had not been adequately warned about the dangers; and their contract had not made provision for compensation in case of harm. All in all, a thoroughly unsatisfactory state of affairs. The company itself, apparently like several others, had been set up by highly respected doctors as a way of generating research funds by contracting with drug companies to test their products using the facilities of their hospital. Their equally eminent colleagues were concerned because it seemed wrong that a profit-making organisation, however laudable the use of the profits, was setting its own ethical standards without reference to an impartial review body. Furthermore, it could be accused of exerting undue influence on the volunteers by offering high payment. The trial was stopped, pending its assessment by the research ethical committee at St Bartholomew's Hospital. ˙

The second case, also in early 1984, involved the government laboratories at Porton Down, where it was revealed somewhat ambiguously by the Defence Secretary, Michael Heseltine, that for 'many years' members of the armed forces had been participating in experiments which were making a 'vital contribution' to Britain's defence against chemical attack. Soldiers, sailors, airmen, medical students are all in a sense captive, just as prisoners are: they may offer their services because the 'reward' could be a reprieve from disciplinary action or a reduced sentence; even students could be participating under some duress if, for instance, they are doing so in order not to displease their chiefs.

Recently, the ABPI has agreed to compensate volunteers who can show they have been damaged by a drug which has been tested before it is used on patients. This is a welcome but limited advance because it does not extend to patients who may have suffered similar damage either in a clinical trial or when the drug is on general sale. These people are obliged to sue through the courts, and even if the drug firm admits liability the victim may get compensation only on the strict condition that the terms of the settlement are not revealed. One firm, E.R. Squibb & Son, has twice imposed this condition on British victims (reported in the *Guardian*, 3 April 1984), thus creating a most undesirable precedent. Although libel claims are frequently settled on this condition, it has never before been the case with a personal injury compensation and it should not be repeated.

There has to be a first time for every advance that is made in medicine. Somebody has to be the first person on whom a new drug or a new technique is tested, and many people will be willing to offer themselves – and the more so the more desperate they are. Heart transplant surgery, test-tube babies and many other extraordinary breakthroughs could not have been achieved without the willing co-operation of such people. Others will do so because they hope to benefit even while knowing that the remedy does not promise cure, and some will do so because they really do want to help others as well as themselves. Provided that patients and volunteers really understand the risk/benefit equation as it applies to them in their individual circumstances and they freely give their informed consent, the human dignity and integrity of these people is not being violated. They are then participating as equals in a common cause – what Ramsey calls 'the great human adventure that is carried forward jointly by the investigator and his subjects'.* Their trust must not be abused, nor their altruism. These human and moral considerations are more important than any scientific advance, and it is these obligations which impose the limits to science.

* Paul Ramsey, *The Patient as Person*, p. 11

Part three
Changing the
perspective

The perspective of needing care is very different from
that of providing it. The first sees the most fundamental
question for patients to be whether they can trust their
care-takers. It requires a stringent adherence to honesty,
in all but a few carefully delineated cases. The second
sees the need to be free to deceive, sometimes for
genuinely humane reasons. It is only by bringing these
perspectives into the open and by considering the
exceptional cases explicitly that the discrepancy can be
reduced and trust restored.

Sissela Bok,
Lying: Moral Choice in Public and Private Life

8 Dilemmas for doctors

> In the grave moral matters of life and death, of maiming
> or curing, of the violation of persons or their bodily
> integrity, a physician or experimenter is more liable to
> make an error in moral judgement if he adopts a policy
> of holding himself open to the possibility that there may
> be significant future permissions to ignore the principle
> of consent than he is if he holds this requirement of an
> informed consent always relevant and applicable.
>
> Paul Ramsey, *The Patient as Person*

A PRINCIPLE AND ITS PRACTICE

Throughout this book we have been examining the issue of
informed consent both as an ethical principle which embodies the
individual's right to self-determination and in its practical
applications, especially in the context of randomised controlled
trials. The widespread and ever-growing use of RCTs as a method
of research in clinical practice is symptomatic of the changing
nature of medicine. The hugely increased store of medical
knowledge gained over the last century has recently been
augmented by some quite spectacular advances in medical
technology. The cumulative effect of these developments has
finally enabled medicine to offer genuine credentials to be
considered as a science rather than art – a status its practitioners
have always yearned for but have hitherto been unable to justify
completely. RCTs, with their emphasis on scientific rigour and
precision for determining the value of treatments rather than the
old hit-or-miss methods (which too often proved to be miss),
appear to enhance and endorse that claim. What we now have to
consider is whether and how the implacable demands of adhering
to scientific method in clinical research can be ethically reconciled

with the still more important obligation to remember that patients are persons who are ends in themselves and can never be treated as means to an end, however necessary that end may appear in the cause of scientific progress.

Crucial to this consideration is the nature and quality of the patient-doctor relationship. Time has not stood still in this respect either. It is a remarkable irony that in former days, when doctors knew far less than they know today and were able to offer little more to their patients than magic potions and a comforting bedside manner, they were held in far greater awe. Today, when everyone generally is better informed (not to be confused with being wiser) doctors, like all other authority figures, have been subjected to considerable criticism and attack. The medical mystique has largely been shattered and the medical profession is finding, often to its acute discomfiture, that its authority is no longer accepted without question and that patients are no longer so ready to prostrate themselves in meek gratitude. Of course, this is not universally true. Many patients in this country are still apparently in awe and therefore passive and uncomplaining. However, psychological studies and plenty of empirical evidence indicate that often it is the most compliant patients who are inwardly seething with hostility and feelings of resentment and suspicion. Unable to express themselves articulately or at least in language which they think doctors expect to hear, unable to frame the questions they want to put, fearful of retribution if they do voice objections, these same patients may nonetheless feel quite desperately that they are being pushed around and treated as objects. This is especially true of hospital patients who are easily and quite understandably overwhelmed by the impersonal atmosphere into which they have been drawn against their will, for no normal person wants to be ill. They feel helpless and taken over – by the system, by the technology and by the bustling, detached professionalism of those caring for them.

The traditional patient-doctor relationship has been fundamentally and irrevocably altered by two factors: medical progress on the one hand, and changes in society's attitudes on the other. What doctors have gained in knowledge they have lost in terms of an empire – their former unchallenged authority. Currently they are floundering about in the unfamiliar and vaguely distasteful role which their own science has thrust upon them: they are seeking to combine their traditional function of being a physician-friend to their actual patients with what they conceive to be their equally important duty to act as a physician-investigator on behalf of future patients. And, it must be said, some of them are not doing too well at either.

Taking the negative aspects first, the old habits of paternalism and benevolent deception, actuated in general by a genuine desire not to harm their patients, die hard even though they are no longer so easy to justify in the face of persistent public scepticism. Doctors feel, quite correctly, that their power and prestige is under threat, and they react defensively to any suggestions that maybe Doctor does not always know best. They find it difficult to relinquish the innate sense of superiority which has been conferred on them by the ancient traditions of their profession and the deference it has previously been accorded. Respect our patients? Why yes, say the best of them, that is what we have always done. But regard them as equals? Expect them to share in the decision-making? Now that is asking too much. Furthermore, they will argue, it is unfair to patients, most of whom do not want to be over-burdened with information, particularly if it is distressing, at a time when their morale is low and their capacity to be rational and objective is sapped by their vulnerable physical condition.

There are other doctors who do not even pretend to such regard for their patients; worse still, they do not perceive that there is any serious conflict of obligation in their dual role. The contempt with which some of these doctors view their patients, and the low opinion they have of their intelligence (often freely expressed within their own circle) makes it comparatively easy for them to justify not seeking informed consent. Since this attitude often goes hand in hand with the belief that it is of paramount importance to get the scientific answers, and if informing their patients means that they are less likely to be co-operative in that research, then such doctors will have no difficulty in asserting that the individual patient's interests must take second place to the interests of science. This is a dangerous road to go down, because if doctors can be allowed to claim immunity from the ethical constraints which are implicit in respecting the individual's autonomy and which the rest of us, though not always conforming to to them, recognise as essential in a civilised society, then science is being allowed to take precedence over morality. As we know from bitter experience, that way leads to man's inhumanity to man, and woman.

On the positive side, trust, and the confidence it engenders, have always been regarded as fundamental to the patient-doctor relationship. Both patients and doctors value it enormously, but as we saw in chapter 2 it is frequently based on an unequal appreciation of its obligations. Doctors who want their patients to trust them but expect them to show that trust by not asking too many questions and by leaving the decision-making in their hands, are disturbed by the idea that they should seek informed consent. Quite understandably they dislike revealing their uncertainties (as they must when seeking informed consent in an RCT); they also fear destroying their patients' confidence in them. It does not seem to occur to them that an honest expression of doubt may actually create trust rather than threaten it, in the same way that it does in so many other human relationships. Although there undoubtedly are some patients who prefer to shut their eyes and hope, most people are not as credulous as this view assumes. There is also quite a lot of evidence to indicate that patients who are not informed may be caused more rather than less stress because they suspect from the reticent demeanour of their doctor and others attending them that they are being kept in the dark, and this makes them exceedingly anxious. What are they keeping from me? Why don't they answer my questions? Unexpressed but keenly felt doubts and worries of this kind can be more threatening to the patient's peace of mind than a frank, kindly discussion opened by the doctor who explains the alternative treatments, why it has been thought necessary to compare them in a controlled trial and why he would like to include this particular patient in the trial. The 'burden of choice' which is thus imposed on the patient and which many doctors believe will cause her unnecessary suffering may in fact be less onerous to bear than the burden of fear endured by so many more patients who suspect that important knowledge is being kept from them.

THE COMMUNICATION GAP

Many of the objections doctors put up against seeking informed consent have more to do with their own shortcomings as communicators than with their patients' inability to comprehend. They complain that patients are prone to misunderstand or forget what they have been told and that many are deluding themselves when they say they want the truth. Of course there will always be some patients who either cannot or will not hear what they are being told, but equally there are many patients who are driven to the brink of despair by the evasions, euphemisms and half-truths that meet their questions. I am reminded of the patient who went to a specialist about her breast lump and after the examination had to persist for twenty minutes in her questioning before she could elicit from him that she need not worry, 'it's not a naughty bump.' He knew what she was asking, she certainly knew what she was asking and had made it as plain as she possibly could, but somehow the doctor simply could not bring himself to utter the dark words 'cancer' or 'tumour', even though, in her case, the news was good.

It is quite true that patients find it difficult to absorb strange and probably unwelcome information, and that the more they get the less they will retain. But what is so surprising about that? In everyday life we have all experienced difficulties in trying to understand unfamiliar material, especially if it is couched in jargon or highly technical language. Often doctors are simply not aware of how obscurely they come over to the lay person.

'This doctor started using all these long Latin words. I said, "Hang on a minute, I don't understand a word you're saying." He said, "Well no, I didn't suppose you would." I said, "Talk English and start again. And just remember it's my body you're talking about." Since then we've had a very good relationship.' Many of us will be able to identify with this patient's frustration but, alas, few have his confidence to tackle their doctors head on and demand a coherent explanation.

The patient who has just been informed that she is seriously ill has been dealt a shattering blow. She needs time to absorb the shock, time to summon up her inner reserves and time to consider how she is going to face the future. To heap on her further complicated information about her participation in a clinical trial may well be confusing and alarming and it is understandable that a compassionate doctor will be reluctant to impose this burden. But the solution to this problem does not lie in pretending that it does not exist. If a doctor thinks that a patient is never really going to understand what she

hears, then it is not the patient whose interests must be sacrificed but
the doctor's interest in the trial – at least as far as that patient is
concerned.

A recent *Lancet* editorial (1982, ii: 78-79) declared that 'if the patient
is not capable of understanding the basic plan of management, he or
she should not be included in the trial.' The writer might have added
that doctors who are incapable of explaining the basic plan, for
whatever reason, should equally be questioning their fitness to be
involved in trials.

Many patients have difficulty in understanding what is being told to
them, not because they are stupid but because they are given scant
time to consider its import. Even if the doctor does not say so in so
many words he makes them feel he is a busy man, too pressured to be
bothered by trifling questions. His body language betrays his
impatience – darting glances at his watch, shuffling papers on his desk,
backing away from the bed as he makes a concluding remark – yet he
may not even be aware how offputting his manner is to the anxious
patient. But if the patient needs time, then the doctor must make time
for her. In most cases it will be time well spent because the patient who
understands is far more likely to cooperate with her future treatment.
Where it concerns explaining a trial and the terms of her participation,
then adequate time *must* be allocated.

A doctor told me he had stopped saying 'is there anything else you'd
like to ask me?' after one patient had been discovered in floods of tears,
distraught because she was convinced that there was more to know
but she did not know what or how to ask him. Apparently, it had not
occured to him that there is an easy way to allay these fears, simply by
prefacing the question with the truthful statement, 'I think I've told
you everything there is to know, but maybe there's something else
you'd like to ask me.'

What about the familiar objection that patients do not really want to
hear the truth, whatever they may say? Doctors who hold this view are
disinclined to give much importance to opinion surveys taken among
a healthy population because they say that nobody knows what they
are going to feel like when they experience serious illness. This must
surely be true of many patients, particularly those who are suddenly
faced with a life-threatening disease. The situation can be just as
fraught in the circumstances of a clinical trial when a doctor realises
that if the patient is to be fully informed then she will have to know that

she has a bad prognosis, at a time when she may not be ready for this information and has given no indication that she wishes to know more than she already knows. Forcing undesired information on a patient is obviously wrong, so what is the doctor to do?

The decision not to seek informed consent should not be left to doctors to deal with on an *ad hoc* basis, yet that is probably precisely what does happen more often than we would like to believe. The permission for doctors to exercise their 'therapeutic privilege' not to tell should come from the ethical committee, and a trial would have to be extraordinarily important to justify such an exemption.

OBTAINING CONSENT

How to obtain informed consent is a real problem for doctors. Verbal explanation through a one-to-one contact between patient and doctor is absolutely essential, but it may not be sufficient to reassure either party that the information has been truly absorbed and understood. Some kind of written consent form which the patient signs to indicate her agreement to the proposed procedure is also necessary to protect the doctor from the risk of later being sued for assault. On the other hand, British doctors rightly abhor the American custom of shoving pages of indigestible and alarming facts about every possible risk and side effect at their patients, the main purpose of which is to protect themselves from charges of malpractice rather than to preserve the rights, and the peace of mind, of the patient.

The patient has to understand that she can resume the dialogue at any time and feel free to ask more questions as they occur to her. Obviously, the doctor cannot always be available for this continuing communication and, indeed, he may not always be the most appropriate person. Much more use could be made of nurse counsellors and other qualified personnel to engage in this task. A suggestion with much to recommend it is that patients who are eligible for entry into a clinical trial should be assigned a 'patient-friend', this person being a doctor other than her own, who is not involved in the trial and is therefore less likely to be unduly prejudiced in its favour.

British consent forms are tersely non-specific to a fault. Although there is no reason why we should expect them to be models of prose style, they ought to avoid alarming solecisms of the kind a friend of mine once found himself signing . . . 'I understand that my operation will not be performed by a particular surgeon.' Those relating to a clinical trial are often particularly misleading in that they may suggest that the treatment will be chosen for the patient when in fact it will be randomly allocated, or they may mention only the treatment to which the patient has already been randomised (see Appendix C for a suggested pro forma for a consent form).

EXPLAINING RANDOMISATION

It has been suggested that a randomised clinical trial is not really research, just a more ethical and scrupulous way of testing treatments.* Therefore, there is no need to explain randomisation – as we have seen, the crucial stumbling block for many doctors – because the patient will not be aware that there is a difference between the doctor who offers the patient a treatment randomly allocated by the computer and the doctor who makes his own 'random' choice from one of several options. In fact, says Brewin, 'A doctor who contributes to randomised treatment trials should not be thought of as a research worker, but simply as a clinician with an ethical duty to his patients not to go on giving them treatments without doing everything possible to assess their true worth.' This may sound fleetingly plausible, but to take this point of view is to ignore a fundamental fact about RCTs. They are designed as research studies; their success depends on ironing out 'irrelevant' variables like the patient's personal preference, and they depend for their statistical significance on being as non-subjective and unbiased as possible. Patients may be crudely matched for certain equivalent disease factors, but if the doctor-investigator started enquiring too closely into the patient's individual circumstances, her background and her personal priorities, this would inevitably influence him in his selection.

An RCT is not meant to be tailored to the patient's needs; the patient is cut to size to fit the RCT, and to pretend anything else is sheer sophistry. The doctor who sincerely believes that, even given this fact, his patient will fare better by entering an RCT than by relying on his unfounded opinion about a treatment, is being honest with himself.

* Thurstan B. Brewin, 'Consent to Randomised Treatment', the *Lancet*, 1982: ii; 919-21

He owes the same duty of honesty and loyalty to his patient who believes that she is in a relationship of trust with him and that everything he does, he does because he believes it to be best for her. The obligation to act as physician-friend must surely take precedence over his interest as physician-investigator to pursue the trial. As we saw in chapter 6, there are some trials in which the fact of randomisation could be a matter of supreme importance to the patient and this is, of course, when it becomes most difficult to explain. Personally I find it hard to understand how any doctor can live with his conscience knowing that he has put patients into a breast cancer trial or any similar study in which patients are likely to have strong preferences or indeed a completely different order of priorities from his own, *without* giving them the opportunity to decide whether they are prepared to accept a randomised allocation of treatments. Truly, this is playing God with a vengeance.

PATERNALISM – IS THERE A CASE FOR IT?

It is almost too easy to accuse doctors of being paternalistic. Of course they are: they always have been, and many of them for most of the time. The difference between then and now is that whereas doctors used to believe that paternalism was what patients needed and expected from them, their confidence today has been shaken, and they feel very sensitive on the subject because they have been so much attacked for it. Doctors argue with some truth that it is all very well for the strong and healthy to cry shame but paternalism is still what the vast majority of their patients thrust upon them. And to a degree we can sympathise with this defence.

There is no doubt that a good patient-doctor relationship is symbiotic; each fulfils an emotional need for the other. The patient seeks reassurance and comfort from her doctor and the doctor needs to feel that the patient respects him and trusts him to use his skills for her benefit. To repeat Ramsey's concept, they are 'joint adventurers in a common cause', the cause of her recovery. Ideally, this is a relationship between equals; patient and doctor are partners working together.

Unfortunately and inescapably, there are many factors, some inherent in the relationship, others brought about by the external circumstances of their encounter, which make it hard to sustain this ideal of equality. Wherever they meet – in the GP's surgery, the out-patient clinic or on the hospital ward – the doctor is surrounded by the trappings of his profession but the patient has little to support her, morally or physically.

In hospital, especially, the regimentation and the deference rippling through the ranks of the hierarchy can swiftly overwhelm the sturdiest spirit. How easy it then becomes for the doctor to assume a paternalistic stance and how difficult it is for the patient to take courage and assert her personal values and her needs as she knows them to be. The shadow cast by medical paternalism is pervasive and infectious. Junior doctors learn their manners from their seniors, ward sisters play up to the consultants, and the patients humbly surrender their bodies for treatment. They are shunted around for various investigations, they take their pills, accept their injections, sign their forms and endeavour to understand what they are being told. The doctor visits them at intervals and is remote and condescending. If all this sounds like a cynical travesty of reality, one has only to hear from doctors themselves their own rueful experiences of becoming a patient to know how painfully true it often is.

What of the substance? The paternalistic doctor acts from the best of motives. He wants to do the best he can for his patient, he wants to protect her from harm and he believes he knows what this 'best' is. Almost invariably this means he is going to lie to her. It may be by giving her a placebo, by postponing or evading altogether the moment of telling her that she has a bad prognosis, by not telling her that there are alternatives to the treatment he has prescribed or by entering her into a clinical trial without seeking her informed consent. Most of the time he will not be caught out in his lies and he will justify his deception by pointing to the pleasing results. The neurotic patient has been pacified by her placebo; the unwitting participant in a trial has received excellent care, has possibly even been lucky enough to be randomised to the treatment which eventually turns out to be the better one; the patient who has been kept ignorant of alternatives has not been tortured by having to make a choice, and so on. Even lying to the terminally ill patient can be justified to his satisfaction because the doctor will say that by doing so he has saved her a few weeks or months of needless anguish. The occasions when the results of the deception turn out badly tend to be brushed aside.

There are several problems about this kind of negative utilitarian paternalism. It works on the principle that the doctor compares two evils and their possible consequences and then decides unilaterally, and taking only his system of values into account, which of the two appears to be the lesser and therefore the 'best' to offer to the patient. Principle is hardly the right word to use in this context because paternalism to this extent evinces scant respect for several moral principles we have already discussed at length. Respect for the individual's autonomy, respect for the truth, respect for keeping promises, respect for justice – all these moral principles are being violated on a scale that we would not tolerate in other circumstances. Is there any reason why we should accept in sickness what we would not dream of accepting in health?

Even judged by the paternalistic doctor's own criteria of consequences, the advantages of paternalism often seem dubious. For example, the dying patient may have been temporarily deceived, but sooner or later she is going to have to know the truth and her last days may be considerably more anguished because she is so angered by the deception or feels bitterly frustrated that she was not given time to carry out final intentions. The patient entered into a clinical trial without her consent may later suspect that this has happened, perhaps through a chance remark she overhears or by comparing her treatment with that of the patient lying in the next bed to her in the ward. Even if she dares not pursue the matter with her doctor, she may still be deeply disturbed by her suspicions and this is not a state of mind conducive to her well-being.

Lies breed lies and the doctor who insists on keeping the truth from a patient involves everyone else round the bedside in a web of deception. Nurses and junior doctors often have serious misgivings about the pretences they are forced to keep up. Relatives who are 'in the secret' find themselves burdened with a dreadful responsibility at a time when their instinct is to share distress and give loving support. Anyone who has been put through a charade of make-believe with a dying relative, whether or not they agreed at the time with the doctor's opinion that this was the best course of action, will know what terrible stresses and tensions are introduced into the relationship by the effort of maintaining the deception. And how, incidentally, are these same people going to react when their own time comes and they remember the lies they were forced to tell? Off-loading the responsibility for knowing the truth onto relatives may ease the doctor's burden, but we also have to question why the rule of confidentiality, so rigidly adhered to in all other patient-doctor interactions, should be waived at this supremely important moment in a patient's life.

Philosophers make a useful distinction between strong and weak paternalism. The strong paternalist is the doctor who adopts a paternalistic attitude towards all his patients on most occasions whereas the weak paternalist is prepared to make decisions on the patient's behalf only in an acutely delicate situation, as when, for example, he decides not to tell the only survivor of an accident that the rest of the family has been killed until she has sufficiently recovered her mental and physical strength to cope with the information.

These examples of medical paternalism illustrate that the problematic moral choices confronting doctors are seldom black and white and always incredibly difficult to resolve. It is far too easy for the outsider to condemn doctors for not telling the truth, particularly in these extreme circumstances. They have an unenviable, depressing task to perform, and it is one which few of us would willingly choose to take over from them. If doctors cannot cure, they want at least to sustain their patients' morale for as long as possible.

But our theme is informed consent and here the real issue is not whether paternalism in itself is right or wrong but whether it can ever be right for patients who have not explicitly stated that they wish to remain uninformed. The reason why so much medical paternalism goes so sadly awry and causes so much distrust and anger is that too often the doctor seems to be looking down the wrong end of the telescope. The paternalist tends to assume that because some patients do want their doctor to make the decisions and do prefer to be kept in ignorance, all patients therefore feel the same way. If we believe that doctors should change their perspective and keep informed consent always as their goal, abandoning it only if the patient clearly signals she does not wish for it, and if we really want doctors to be honest with us, then we must be equally clearsighted about our own objections and equally honest with them. We have to explain what our perspective is and be sure that we understand the full implications of being responsible for making our own choices. This done, we have every right to enjoin on doctors their duty to respect our wishes and abide by our decisions.

9 Whose body is it?

> We live in an era where the accepted wisdom is that
> nothing of any consequence can be explained to the
> general public. They are regarded as pleasure-soddened
> morons, who have to strain their brain-box to tell the
> difference between butter and margarine. This
> contemptuous view of the average citizen appears to co-
> exist quite happily with the knowledge that ultimate
> political power rests in his or her hands ... Difficult
> issues can be explained. What it takes is time and trouble.
> Brian Walden, *Evening Standard*, 9 August 1983

THE POLITICS OF CONTEMPT

Brian Walden, the political journalist, coined this phrase to
describe the arrogant behaviour of so many politicians who,
having spent a great deal of time and energy wooing us for our
vote, then proceed to smack us in the face by denying us our
democratic right to participate in any meaningful way in the
decisions which affect our lives. Others have made the same point.
'We have the right to vote, but not to know,' wrote Peter Jenkins
in the *Guardian* on 28 March 1984, enlarging on Richard
Crossman's pithy comment many years ago that secrecy is the
endemic English disease. Helpless bystanders, we see our rights
being eroded all the time by those in the high places of power and
authority. Politics, the Civil Service, big business, the law and
medicine are all zones of influence thickly hedged about by
restrictive practices which effectively put them out of bounds to
the average citizen. It requires an enormous amount of persistence
and commitment to break into them, and those who do so
invariably suffer abuse, a bloody nose and worse for their pains.

Take the long-running saga of Depo-Provera, the injectable
long-term contraceptive. For almost twenty years this drug has

been used on millions of Third World women, but it was only after a few women in this country, alarmed by the distressing and acutely uncomfortable symptoms it produced (including prolonged heavy bleeding), organised themselves into a co-ordinating group to collect and report on case histories that 'the authorities' began to take notice of the complaints. When finally convinced by the evidence, the DHSS, to give it its due, responded with uncharacteristic alacrity by overruling the CSM and refusing to license the drug. Uproar from Upjohn, the manufacturers, who claimed, naturally, that the drug was of inestimable benefit in preventing unwanted pregnancies and that the risks were far outweighed by the drug's reliability. A panel of experts, led by Dame Josephine Barnes, an eminent gynaecologist and former president of the BMA, was speedily enlisted to give evidence in the drug's favour. Dame Josephine protested hotly to the Health Minister, Kenneth Clarke, that any suggestion that the drug might be abused by doctors who were giving it mainly to women deemed irresponsible and of low intelligence was 'tantamount to saying that doctors in this country are unreliable and act unethically'. At the public hearing in April 1983 she was obliged to admit that the consent forms provided by various health authorities were inadequate and that women were not being properly informed about the side effects. The women's co-ordinating group, which was not allowed to speak at the hearing, was accused by Upjohn's QC, Mr Christopher Bathhurst, of being authoritarian in its demand that the drug should be banned and that it was interfering with women's right to choose! The Health Minister remained unimpressed by Upjohn's appeal and refused to revoke the ban until his own panel of experts had investigated the evidence.

A year later that panel, chaired by Professor Rosalind Hurley, has concluded that the drug may be administered but only as a last resort and with the most stringent precautions. The report is adamant about the necessity for informed consent, and it outlines in precise detail the measures to be taken, both by the manufacturers and doctors, to ensure that women fully understand to what they are consenting. A further disturbing conclusion to emerge from the panel's investigations is that the drug 'has not been subject to good quality research' and that there are some indications, not yet convincingly disproved, to suggest that it could be linked with certain cancers. In a written Commons answer, the Minister has made it clear that Depo-Provera must no longer be given to those women least able to protect themselves because for whatever reason – educational, social or cultural – they are unable to understand the full implications of taking the drug.

The final outcome of this story is a triumphant vindication of the patient's right to informed consent, and its unsung heroines are those much-vilified women who refused to be deterred by the heavy guns mustered against them. They have won an important battle for us all, but especially for the vulnerable, most easily exploited members of the population. Women in the Third World are not so fortunate because the restrictions on Depo-Provera apply only in this country. And it is, of course, in the Third World, where post-marketing surveillance and follow-up studies of drugs are most needed, that they are least likely to be pursued with any diligence.

Here is another disturbing story. An article in *World Medicine* on 26 November 1983, which was taken up by the *Evening Standard* two days later, revealed that women were undergoing vaginal examinations under anaesthetic without their consent. This is apparently a common practice in teaching hospitals to enable medical students to learn their skills – which could explain why some fully fledged doctors are unable to do an internal examination on their conscious patients without making them flinch. Legally this practice constitutes assault (unauthorised touching), but there is no indication that the medical profession is hastening to adopt an alternative teaching method. An indignant letter from a Dr Margaret Puxon in the correspondence columns of *World Medicine* on 21 January 1984 deplored the revelation because 'public opinion is easily whipped up by reference to sexual organs'; she asked how students can be expected to acquire their clinical experience if they are not allowed to practise these and other essential examination skills on 'diseased as well as normal patients'. A valid point, but once again we have to ask her and other doctors who hold the same opinion why they think the sick should be deprived of the rights they normally expect to exercise when they are well? She concludes her letter with the threatening inference that if informed consent is going to be necessary for these procedures, and if this means that large numbers of patients will refuse, then 'it might well be necessary for clinicians to consider whether to admit patients on such terms'.

This attitude betrays a degree of lofty, high-handed scorn for members of the general public who dare to voice a legitimate anxiety. We must hope it is aberrant rather than typical of the medical profession as a whole, but that it exists at all in the 1980s is serious cause for concern. When George Bernard Shaw fired off his famous diatribe against the profession eighty years ago in his preface to *The Doctor's Dilemma*, one of the main burdens of his complaint was that doctors were corrupted by their need to exact fees for their services from their patients, leading them to indulge in unnecessary and extensive procedures for the rich and to neglect the poor: Today, when many of his socialist ideals for a state-run medical service have materialised – although certainly not as completely or as successfully as he would have hoped – it is intensely disturbing to realise that patients have hardly got beyond the first post in the struggle to establish their rights. It is alarming but true that we seem to be moving backwards into a situation in which the price that NHS patients pay for getting 'free' medicine is that they are deprived of choice and a voice.

The NHS was founded on a high tide of idealism to enable everyone in the community to have equal access to the medical care and services they need, regardless of their means or social status. It is essential to remind ourselves that our health care is not free; we pay for it through our taxes, but we are obliged to rely on those who administrate it and those who govern us to determine the standards of that service and to decide on priorities. Currently 5½ per cent of the Gross National Product is allocated to the health budget, and that makes it one of the cheapest health systems in the European Community. (France and Germany each apportion 8 per cent and in America and Sweden it is as high as 9½ per cent). Given that it is so severely underfunded, the NHS still manages to give remarkable value for money. But, as we saw in chapter 2, the capital cake is unevenly distributed and too much of it goes on 'glamour' treatments which require high technology and intensive specialised care at the expense of the chronically sick, the disabled and the old. Acute medicine attracts money for research and prestige for doctors whereas the Cinderella specialities like geriatrics and psychiatry are desperately short of both. The inequities lie not only in what is offered to whom but also in where services are available. In some parts of the country waiting lists for necessary but not life-saving operations such as hysterectomies or hip replacements stretch into years. Private medicine is on the increase and private patients are the only people to have any real clout with their doctors. If you want to exercise your right to choice it seems you have to pay for it.

Is it any wonder that in all this demoralising muddle and mayhem, which has less to do with economic straits than with the dire lack of vision and conviction of most of those who govern us, the notion that patients have a right to informed consent has come to be regarded in certain quarters as something of an idle luxury? 'Give us more time, more money and less hassle and then maybe we can sit down and work this thing out', groan the sorely tried doctors. Others of a more cynical cast of mind regard it as a mere fashionable whim which has regrettably found its way across the Atlantic and which they hope to banish quietly by keeping their heads down and avoiding paying it too much attention. If, however, in the course of reading this book you have become convinced that enabling patients to give their informed consent for treatment, whether it be in ordinary clinical practice or in clinical trials, is neither a concession nor a courtesy to be granted by well-disposed doctors as and when they see fit, but an inalienable human right which safeguards our personal integrity, then perhaps you will also agree that the time has come to insist that our claim to this right be honoured.

A PATIENT'S BILL OF RIGHTS

The American Hospital Association produced the first Bill of Rights for patients in 1973 (see Appendix B). Although this particular document has no legal standing, it has subsequently been used as a model by several governmental bodies in North America which have adopted legally binding bills of rights. In January 1984, the European Parliament formally tabled a Resolution inviting the Commission to submit as soon as possible a proposal for a European Charter on the Rights of Patients (see Appendix B). The language of this Resolution and the report of the discussions leading up to it are urgent and unequivocal. Among the fifteen rights it stresses must be incorporated in the Charter are (f) 'the right to information concerning diagnosis, therapy and prognosis, the patient's right of access to his [or her] own medical data, and the patient's right to give his [or her] consent to or to refuse the treatment proposed' and (i) 'the right to complaint based on "damage to the interests of the patient".'

A Bill of Rights is much stronger than a code. It is far more than a set of guidelines for recommended ethical behaviour, which in most cases has been drawn up by a professional body as much to protect its own interests as those of the clients it exists to serve. A Bill of Rights, a Charter, call it what you will, defines certain human rights based on moral principles which must be recognised and honoured. Once these rights have been enshrined by a sovereign body in a written statement, and even though they are not legally binding in themselves, we can and must urge our own Parliament to endorse them by producing the appropriate legislation. If our rights are not upheld by the law we remain powerless, because then we can neither claim redress if they are infringed in our respect nor is there any binding duty for others to observe them on our behalf, beyond the individual's private sense of moral obligation. As we have seen, this can only too easily be suspended by special pleading for 'special cases'.

There are, I am glad to say, many doctors who support the idea of a Bill of Rights for Patients, but there are others, equally committed to placing their patients' welfare above the interests of science or their personal advancement, who nonetheless maintain that their relationship with patients is too delicate to be governed by the law. But is there any reason to suppose that this important human relationship can be put above the law when other similarly delicate human relationships like those between wife and husband, child and parent, employee and employer, are all subject to the law? Patients, more almost than any other group in the population, need legal safeguards to protect their rights and interests precisely *because* their condition puts them into an acutely vulnerable position where their trust can easily be abused by unscrupulous or misguided doctors.

The example of vaginal examinations performed under anaesthetic without the patient's consent has already been cited, but there are many other investigations – some more and some less invasive – to which patients may be subjected without being told that they are not strictly necessary for them and without, of course, their permission being sought. For instance, they may be asked to give regular urine samples or supply blood, or they may be used as 'controls' in a clinical trial; the information gained from these procedures is made available to researchers engaged on a study which is quite unrelated to the patient's own condition. If a patient does not know that this is the purpose of the investigation then this constitutes an assault. The patient who does ask and then refuses to comply may well be regarded as 'difficult'. Probably most patients would be happy to surrender something as untaxing as their body fluids in the cause of research, but those who are not and who certainly would not be willing to co-operate in something more drastic have every right to have their wishes respected. Not to grant this respect by not asking for the patient's informed consent is to make the patient, her body and her history, the property of the medical profession to use as they wish. This is a very murky area in medical practice and one about which most patients are quite unaware, yet ethically, informed consent is quite as necessary here as it is for other forms of treatment.

Beecher has said that the patient's 'great safeguard in experimentation as in therapy is the presence of the skillful, informed, intelligent, honest, responsible, compassionate physician', and this of course is true. But it simply is not a strong enough safeguard for us to rely upon exclusively.* For one thing the individual doctor may not be as autonomous as either he or the patient would like to imagine. Doctors participating in trials take decisions on their patients' behalf in order to satisfy the demands of the trial protocol. The researchers controlling the trials are distanced from the day-to-day care of the patients; they argue that they need the information to inform other doctors but they themselves are not directly responsible for managing the patients. Quite easily a situation develops where power is wielded by remote control and no one is personally accountable.

The idea that the patient-doctor relationship should be regarded as a contract has always been shunned by doctors who fear and distrust the legalistic implications of the term, but if we think of it as a partnership mutually entered into – which it is – then, like any joint agreement or pact – it should be underwritten by certain accepted obligations on both sides. The trust between patient and doctor will be enhanced rather than destroyed by this shared understanding.

---

* Henry K. Beecher, 'Consent in Clinical Experimentation: Myth and Reality', *Journal of the American Medical Association*, 1966, 195; 1: 34–35

NO RIGHTS WITHOUT RESPONSIBILITIES

Throughout this book I have concentrated on the duties and responsibilities of doctors towards their patients, particularly in the matter of respecting their right as autonomous persons to give informed consent, for this I believe is crucial to creating an ethical and healthy patient-doctor relationship. I have viewed this issue from a perspective which I hope and believe is shared by the majority of patients, past, present and potential. But if patients have rights in health care, they also have responsibilities. Some of these patient obligations we have already touched upon, like our duty to confide honestly in our doctors and our duty not to make unreasonable demands either on them or other health professionals who have obligations to other patients aside from ourselves. These are ways in which patients can express their respect for persons.

If we want that respect to be reciprocated for ourselves and if we consider it to be embodied in the principle of informed consent, then we must recognise the measure of responsibility we are assuming by demanding that right. Not always, of course, but in certain circumstances, the information we are given may be deeply distressing; the choices presented to us may emerge as deeply unpalatable; the decisions facing us could be the hardest we will ever have to make in our whole lives. Giving our informed consent to medical treatment is the ultimate expression of the responsibility each one of us has for our own person. If we do not like what it involves, then we are perfectly entitled to ask our doctors to take over the full responsibility of decision-making. But if we insist on being informed and deciding for ourselves, then we have no right and no reason later to turn round and blame the doctors who have complied with our request to determine our own fate.

Our bodies belong to us. They are who we are. The person we are reposes in their material form. When we need medical attention or can no longer care for our bodies ourselves, we share some part of our personal responsibility with our doctors but we do not cede it entirely. We alone must decide how we wish to be treated, whether to be a fully informed participant or to place ourselves unreservedly in the hands of our doctors. We alone must decide whether we wish to lend our bodies to the cause of medical research. No one has the right to deprive us of the opportunity of knowing that we are making this supremely generous gesture on behalf of future generations. Nor does anyone have the right to seek to influence, deceive or manipulate us into making a decision which is against our own best wishes for ourselves. We have the right to expect that our human dignity and integrity, the beliefs, values and interests that make each one of us a unique person, will never cease to be respected, whatever our physical or mental state. We have a duty to respect other persons as we wish them to respect us and as we respect ourselves and our bodies.

Appendix A

THE HIPPOCRATIC OATH

I swear by Apollo the physician, and Aesculapius and Health, and All-heal, and all the gods and goddesses, that, according to my ability and judgement, I will keep this Oath and this stipulation – to reckon him who taught me this Art equally dear to me as my parents, to share my substance with him, and relieve his necessities if required; to look upon his offspring in the same footing as my own brothers, and to teach them this Art, if they shall wish to learn it, without fee or stipulation; and that by precept, lecture and every other mode of instruction, I will impart a knowledge of the Art to my own sons, and those of my teachers, and to disciples bound by a stipulation and oath according to the law of medicine, but to none other. I will follow that system of regimen which, according to my ability and judgement, I consider for the benefit of my patients, and abstain from whatever is deleterious and mischievous. I will give no deadly medicine to anyone if asked, nor suggest any such counsel; and in like manner I will not give to a woman a pessary to produce abortion. With purity and holiness I will pass my life and practise my Art. I will not cut persons labouring under the stone, but will leave this to be done by men who are practitioners of this art. Into whatever houses I enter, I will go into them for the benefit of the sick, and will abstain from every voluntary act of mischief and corruption; and, further, from the seduction of females, or males, of freemen or slaves. Whatever, in connection with my professional practice, or not in connection with it, I see or hear, in the life of men, which ought not to be spoken abroad, I will not divulge, as reckoning that all such should be kept secret. While I continue to keep this oath unviolated, may it be granted to me to enjoy life and the practice of the Art, respected by all men, in all times. But should I trespass and violate this Oath, may the reverse be my lot.

THE DECLARATION OF GENEVA (1968)

At the time of being admitted as a Member of the Medical Profession:

> I solemnly pledge myself to consecrate my life to the service of humanity;
>
> I will give to my teachers the respect and gratitude which is their due;
>
> I will practise my profession with conscience and dignity;
>
> The health of my patient will be my first consideration;
>
> I will respect the secrets which are confided in me, even after the patient has died;
>
> I will maintain by all the means in my power, the honour and noble traditions of the medical profession;
>
> My colleagues will be my brothers;
>
> I will not permit considerations of religion, nationality, race, party politics or social standing to intervene between my duty and my patients;
>
> I will maintain the utmost respect for human life from the time of conception; even under threat, I will not use my medical knowledge contrary to the laws of humanity;
>
> I make these promises solemnly, freely and upon my honour.

THE NUREMBERG CODE

Permissible medical experiments

The great weight of the evidence before us is to the effect that certain types of medical experiments on human beings, when kept within reasonably well-defined bounds, conform to the ethics of the medical profession generally. The protagonists of the practice of human experimentation justify their view on the basis that such experiments yield results for the good of society that are unprocurable by other methods or means of study. All agree, however, that certain basic principles must be observed in order to satisfy moral, ethical and legal concepts:

1. The voluntary consent of the human subject is absolutely essential. This means that the person involved should have legal capacity to give consent; should be so situated as to be able to exercise free power of choice, without the intervention of any element of force, fraud, deceit, duress, overreaching, or other ulterior form of constraint or coercion; and should have sufficient knowledge and comprehension of the elements of the subject matter involved as to enable him to make an understanding and enlightened decision. This latter element requires that before the acceptance of an affirmative decision by the experimental subject there should be made known to him the nature, duration, and purpose of the experiment; the method and means by which it is to be conducted; all inconveniences and hazards reasonably to be expected; and the effects upon his health or person which may possibly come from his participation in the experiment.

   The duty and responsibility for ascertaining the quality of the consent rests upon each individual who initiates, directs, or engages in the experiment. It is a personal duty and responsibility which may not be delegated to another with impunity.

2. The experiment should be such as to yield fruitful results for the good of society, unprocurable by other methods or means of study, and not random and unnecessary in nature.

3. The experiment should be so designed and based on the results of animal experimentation and a knowledge of the natural history of the disease or other problem under study that the anticipated results justify the performance of the experiment.

4. The experiment should be so conducted as to avoid all unnecessary physical and mental suffering and injury.

5. No experiment should be conducted where there is an *a priori* reason to believe that death or disabling injury will occur; except, perhaps, in those experiments where the experimental physicians also serve as the subjects.

6. The degree of risk to be taken should never exceed that determined by the humanitarian importance of the problem to be solved by the experiment.

7. Proper preparations should be made, and adequate facilities provided to protect the experimental subject against even remote possibilities of injury, disability, or death.

8. The experiment should be conducted only by scientifically

qualified persons. The highest degree of skill and care should be required through all stages of the experiment of those who conduct or engage in the experiment.

9. During the course of the experiment the human subject should be at liberty to bring the experiment to an end if he has reached the physical or mental state where continuation of the experiment seems to him to be impossible.

10. During the course of the experiment the scientist in charge must be prepared to terminate the experiment at any stage, if he has probable cause to believe, in the exercise of the good faith, superior skill, and careful judgment required of him, that a continuation of the experiment is likely to result in injury, disability, or death to the experimental subject.

DECLARATION OF HELSINKI (1975)

It is the mission of the medical doctor to safeguard the health of the people. His or her knowledge and conscience are dedicated to the fulfilment of this mission.

The Declaration of Geneva of the World Medical Association binds the doctor with the words, 'The health of my patient will be my first consideration', and the International Code of Medical Ethics declares that 'Any act or advice which could weaken physical or mental resistance of a human being may be used only in his interest.'

The purpose of biomedical research involving human subjects must be to improve diagnostic, therapeutic and prophylactic procedures and the understanding of the aetiology and pathogenesis of disease.

In current medical practice most diagnostic, therapeutic or prophylactic procedures involve hazards. This applies *a fortiori* to biomedical research.

Medical progress is based on research which ultimately must rest in part on experimentation involving human subjects. In the field of biochemical research a fundamental distinction must be recognised between medical research in which the aim is essentially diagnostic or therapeutic for a patient, and medical research, the essential object of which is purely scientific and without direct diagnostic or therapeutic value to the person subjected to the research.

Special caution must be exercised in the conduct of research which may affect the environment, and the welfare of animals used for research must be respected.

Because it is essential that the results of laboratory experiments be applied to human beings to further scientific knowledge and to help suffering humanity, the World Medical Association has prepared the following recommendations as a guide to every doctor in biomedical research involving human subjects. They should be kept under review in the future. It must be stressed that the standards as drafted are only a guide to physicians all over the world. Doctors are not relieved from criminal, civil and ethical responsibilities under the laws of their own countries.

I Basic Principles

1. Biomedical research involving human subjects must conform to generally accepted scientific principles and should be based on adequately performed laboratory and animal experimentation and on a thorough knowledge of the scientific literature.
2. The design and performance of each experimental procedure involving human subjects should be clearly formulated in an experimental protocol which should be transmitted to a specially appointed independent committee for consideration, comment and guidance.
3. Biomedical research involving human subjects should be conducted only by scientifically qualified persons and under the supervision of a clinically competent medical person. The responsibility for the human subject must always rest with the medically qualified person and never rest on the subject of the research, even though the subject has given his or her consent.
4. Biomedical research involving human subjects cannot legitimately be carried out unless the importance of the objective is in proportion to the inherent risk to the subject.
5. Every biomedical research project involving human subjects should be preceded by careful assessment of predictable risks in comparison with foreseeable benefits to the subject or to others. Concern for the interest of the subject must always prevail over the interests of science and society.
6. The right of the research subject to safeguard his or her integrity must always be respected. Every precaution should be taken to respect the privacy of the subject and to minimize the impact of the study on the subject's physical and mental integrity and on the personality of the subject.
7. Doctors should abstain from engaging in research projects involving human subjects unless they are satisfied that the hazards involved are believed to be predictable. Doctors should cease any investigation if the hazards are found to outweigh

the potential benefits.

8. In publication of the results of his or her research, the doctor is obliged to preserve the accuracy of the results. Reports of experimentation not in accordance with the principles laid down in this Declaration should not be accepted for publication.

9. In any research on human beings, each potential subject must be adequately informed of the aims, methods, anticipated benefits and potential hazards of the study and the discomfort it may entail. He or she should be informed that he or she is at liberty to abstain from participation in the study and that he or she is free to withdraw his or her consent to participation at any time. The doctor should then obtain the subject's freely-given informed consent, preferably in writing.

10. When obtaining informed consent for the research project the doctor should be particularly cautious if the subject is in a dependent relationship to him or her or may consent under duress. In that case the informed consent should be obtained by a doctor who is not engaged in the investigation and who is completely independent of this official relationship.

11. In the case of legal incompetence, informed consent should be obtained from the legal guardian in accordance with national legislation. Where physical or mental incapacity makes it impossible to obtain informed consent, or when the subject is a minor, permission from the responsible relative replaces that of the subject in accordance with national legislation.

12. The research protocol should always contain a statement of the ethical considerations involved and should indicate that the principles enunciated in the present Declaration are complied with.

II Medical Research Combined with Professional Care (Clinical Research)

1. In the treatment of the sick person, the doctor must be free to use a new diagnostic and therapeutic measure, if in his or her judgment it offers hope of saving life, re-establishing health or alleviating suffering.

2. The potential benefits, hazards and discomfort of a new method should be weighed against the advantages of the best current diagnostic and therapeutic methods.

3. In any medical study, every patient –including those of a control group, if any– should be assured of the best proven diagnostic and therapeutic method.

4. The refusal of the patient to participate in a study must never interfere with the doctor-patient relationship.
5. If the doctor considers it essential not to obtain informed consent, the specific reasons for this proposal should be stated in the experimental protocol for transmission to the independent committee. (I.2)
6. The doctor can combine medical research with professional care, the objective being the acquisition of new medical knowledge, only to the extent that medical research is justified by its potential diagnostic or therapeutic value for the patient.

III Non-Therapeutic Biomedical Research Involving Human Subjects (Non-clinical Biomedical Research)

1. In the purely scientific application of medical research carried out on a human being, it is the duty of the doctor to remain the protector of the life and health of that person on whom biomedical research is being carried out.
2. The subjects should be volunteers – either healthy persons or patients for whom the experimental design is not related to the patient's illness.
3. The investigator or the investigating team should discontinue the research if in his/her or their judgement it may, if continued, be harmful to the individual.
4. In research on man, the interest of science and society should never take precedence over considerations related to the well-being of the subject.

The World Medical Association has produced four other important statements as follows:

The Declaration of Sydney (1968) – a statement on death.

The Declaration of Oslo (1970) – a statement on therapeutic abortion.

The Declaration of Tokio (1975) – guidelines for medical doctors concerning torture and other cruel, inhuman or degrading treatment or punishment in relation to detention and imprisonment.

The Declaration of Hawaii (1977) – guidelines for psychiatrists.

For the full text of these and other codes see *The BMA Handbook of Medical Ethics*.

Appendix B

AMERICAN HOSPITAL ASSOCIATION – A PATIENT'S BILL OF RIGHTS

The American Hospital Association presents a Patient's Bill of Rights with the expectation that observance of these rights will contribute to more effective patient care and greater satisfaction for the patient, his physician, and the hospital organization. Further, the Association presents these rights in the expectation that they will be supported by the hospital on behalf of its patients, as an integral part of the healing process. It is recognized that a personal relationship between the physician and the patient is essential for the provision of proper medical care. The traditional physician-patient relationship takes on a new dimension when care is rendered within an organizational structure. Legal precedent has established that the institution itself also has a responsibility to the patient. It is in recognition of these factors that these rights are affirmed.

1. The patient has the right to considerate and respectful care.
2. The patient has the right to obtain from his physician complete current information concerning his diagnosis, treatment, and prognosis in terms the patient can be reasonably expected to understand. When it is not medically advisable to give such information to the patient, the information should be made available to an appropriate person on his behalf. He has the right

to know, by name, the physician responsible for coordinating his care.

3. The patient has the right to receive from his physician information necessary to give informed consent prior to the start of any procedure and/or treatment. Except in emergencies, such information for informed consent should include but not necessarily be limited to the specific procedure and/or treatment, the medically significant risks involved, and the probable duration of incapacitation. Where medically significant alternatives for care or treatment exist, or when the patient requests information concerning medical alternatives, the patient has the right to know the name of the person responsible for the procedures and/or treatment.

4. The patient has the right to refuse treatment to the extent permitted by law and to be informed of the medical consequences of his action.

5. The patient has the right to every consideration of his privacy concerning his own medical care program. Case discussion, consultation, examination, and treatment are confidential and should be conducted discreetly. Those not directly involved in his care must have the permission of the patient to be present.

6. The patient has the right to expect that within its capacity a hospital must make reasonable response to the request of a patient for services. The hospital must provide evaluation, service, and/or referral as indicated by the urgency of the case. When medically permissible, a patient may be transferred to another facility only after he has received complete information and explanation concerning the needs for and alternatives to such a transfer. The institution to which the patient is to be transferred must first have accepted the patient for transfer.

8. The patient has the right to obtain information as to any relationship of his hospital to other health care and educational institutions insofar as his care is concerned. The patient has the right to obtain information as to the existence of any professional relationships among individuals, by name, who are treating him.

9. The patient has the right to be advised if the hospital proposes to engage in or perform human experimentation affecting his care or treatment. The patient has the right to refuse to participate in such research projects.

10. The patient has the right to expect reasonable continuity of care.

He has the right to know in advance what appointment times and physicians are available and where. The patient has the right to expect that the hospital will provide a mechanism whereby he is informed by his physician or a delegate of the physician of the patient's continuing health care requirements following discharge.

11. The patient has the right to examine and receive an explanation of his bill regardless of source of payment.

12. The patient has the right to know what hospital rules and regulations apply to his conduct as a patient.

No catalog of rights can guarantee for the patient the kind of treatment he has a right to expect. A hospital has many functions to perform, including the prevention and treatment of disease, the education of both health professionals and patients, and the conduct of clinical research. All these activities must be conducted with an overriding concern for the patient, and, above all, the recognition of his dignity as a human being. Success in achieving this recognition assures success in the defense of the rights of the patient.

[Approved by the American Hospital Asociation of Delegates, 6 February 1973.]

RESOLUTION ON A EUROPEAN CHARTER ON THE RIGHTS OF PATIENTS

(a) the right to available treatment and care appropriate to the illness

(b) the right to prompt treatment

(c) the right to adequate social security cover to allow the rights set out in (a) to be exercised

(d) the right to free choice of medical practitioner and health-care establishment

(e) the right of access to hospital service within a reasonable travelling distance

(f) the right to information concerning diagnosis, therapy and prognosis, the patient's right of access to his own medical data, and the patient's right to give his consent to or refuse the treatment proposed

(g) the right to medical confidentiality, the only possible

exceptions to which should be on a limited number of serious and well-defined grounds, having due regard for the integrity of the human person

(h) the patient's right to lift the obligation of confidentiality completely or in part as regards his own medical records

(i) the right to complaint based on 'damage to the interests of the patient'

(j) the right to an appeal procedure before the courts

(k) the rights and duties of medical practitioners

(l) the patient's right to be represented by independent associations and organisations

(m) the definition of the legal status of the patient in a health-care establishment

(n) the right to respect for private life and for religious and philosophical convictions

(o) the right to a dignified death.

4. Considers that it may be necessary, in certain well-defined circumstances, to limit the rights of patients where they would involve a danger to public health

5. Is of the opinion that the specific problems pertaining to the rights of the mentally ill and of children should not be dealt with in this context but in a special charter

[Extract from RESOLUTION tabled by the European Parliament on 19 January 1984 and forwarded by the President to the Commission with the instruction to submit as soon as possible a European Charter on the Rights of Patients]

Appendix C

SUGGESTED PRO FORMA FOR PATIENT'S OR VOLUNTEER'S
INFORMED CONSENT TO PARTICIPATION IN A CLINICAL TRIAL

You are invited to participate in a study of (state what is being studied).
We hope to learn (state what the study is designed to discover or
establish). You were selected as a possible participant in this study
because (state why the subject was selected).

If you decide to participate, we (or: Dr — and his associates) will
(describe the procedures, including the use of placebos, to be
followed, including their purposes, how long they will take, and their
frequency). If placebos are to be used the term should be explained in
simple language. (Describe the discomforts and inconveniences
reasonably to be expected. An estimate of the total time required must
be included.) (Describe the risks reasonably to be expected.)
(Describe any benefits reasonably to be expected.) If benefits are
mentioned, add: We cannot and do not guarantee or promise that you
will receive any benefits from this study.

(Describe appropriate alternative procedures that might be advan-
tageous to the subject, if any. Any standard treatment that is being
withheld must be disclosed.)

Any information that is obtained in connection with this study and
that can be identified with you will remain confidential and will be
disclosed only with your permission. If you give us your permission
by signing this document, we plan to disclose (state the persons or

agencies to whom the information will be furnished, the nature of the information to be furnished, and the purpose of the disclosure.)

(If the subject will receive remuneration, describe the amount or nature.) (If there is a possibility of additional costs to the subject because of participation, describe it.)

Your decision whether or not to participate will not prejudice your future relations with the (Institution) (and the named cooperating institution, if any). If you decide to participate you are free to withdraw your consent and to discontinue participation at any time without prejudice.

If you have any questions, we expect you to ask us. If you have any additional questions later, Dr —, (give a phone number or address) will be happy to answer them.

[Extracted from paper by Campbell, J.D. and McEwin, K., entitled 'The Hospital Ethics Committee' first presented at the Symposium on the Ethical and Legal Problems associated with Clinical Trials held in Canberra, 27 June 1980 and published in *Medical Journal of Australia*, 1981, 1: 168–169.]

Chapter references

1. Informed consent – what are we talking about?

Ursula Brandt, 'An American viewpoint on informed consent' in: M. Baum, R Kay and H. Scheurlen (eds), *Clinical Trials in Early Breast Cancer*, 2nd Heidelberg Symposium, Heidelberg, 14-17 December 1981, pp. 293-99.

Ruth B. Kraft, 'The breast cancer controversy and its implications for the informed consent doctrine', *Journal of Legal Medicine*, 2 (1980), pp. 47–84.

2. Informed consent – the right to know

Tom L. Beauchamp and James F. Childress, *Principles of Biomedical Ethics*, Oxford University Press, Oxford, 1979.

M. Cranston, *What Are Human Rights?*, Bodley Head, London, 1974.

Jonathan Glover, *Causing Death and Saving Lives*, Pelican, London, 1977.

Robert M. Veatch, *A Theory of Medical Ethics*, Basic Books Inc., New York, 1981.

3. Understanding consent – the right to say no

Charles M. Culver and Bernard Gert, *Philosophy in Medicine*, Oxford University Press, Oxford, 1982.

Hon. Mr Justice M.D. Kirby, 'Informed Consent: what does it mean?', *Journal of Medical Ethics*, 9, 2 (1983), pp. 69-75.

Helga Kuhse, 'A Modern Myth. That letting die is not the intentional causation of death: some reflections on the trial and acquittal of Dr Leonard Arthur', *Journal of Applied Philosophy*, 1, 1 (1984), pp. 21–38.

B. Mahendra, 'Some ethical issues in dementia research', *Journal of Medical Ethics*, 1 (1984), pp. 29-31.

Margaret Somerville, *Consent to Medical Care*, Law Commission of Canada, Ottawa, 1979. (Study paper prepared for the Law Reform Commission of Canada, Protection of Life series.)

4. Codes and laws

The Belmont Report – Ethical Principles and guidelines for the protection of human subjects and research, ed. National Commission for the Protection of Human Subjects and Biomedical and Behavioral Research, DHEW Publications no ( ) S, 78-0012, US Government Printing Office, Washington D.C. (1978), pp. 4-8.

Diana Brahams, 'The need for consent in medical trials', *New Law Journal* (15 July 1982), p. 687.

British Medical Association, *The Handbook of Medical Ethics*, BMA, London, 1981.

B.A. Bunker, 'Discarded operations: surgical innovation by trial and error' in: J.P. Bunker, B.A. Barnes and F. Mosteller (eds), *Costs, Risks and Benefits of Surgery*, Oxford University Press, New York, 1977, pp. 109-23.

Cancer Research Campaign working party in breast conservation, 'Informed consent: ethical, legal and medical implications for doctors and patients who participate in randomised clinical trials', *British Medical Journal*, 286 (1983), pp. 1117-21.

Victor Herbert, 'Informed Consent – a legal evaluation', *Cancer*, 46 (1980), pp. 1042-44.

Michael A. Jones, 'Medical Negligence –the burden of proof', *New Law Journal* (6 January 1984), pp. 7-9.

Jay Katz (ed), *Experimentation with Human Beings*, New York, 1972.

Legal correspondent, 'Consent to medical treatment', *British Medical Journal*, 278 (1979), pp. 1091-92.

Legal correspondent, 'Consent to treatment: the medical standard reaffirmed', *British Medical Journal*, 288 (1984), pp. 802-03.

Charles J. Lewis, 'Consenting to an operation: the surgeon's duty of disclosure', *The Law Society's Gazette* (October 1983), pp. 2667-71.

Charles J. Lewis, 'The surgeon's duty of disclosure: recent developments', *The Law Society's Gazette* (June 1984), pp. 1827-29.

J.K. Mason and R.A. McCall Smith, *Law and Medical Ethics*, Butterworths, London, 1983.

Medical Research Council, *Responsibility in Investigations on Human Subjects*, HMSO, Cmnd 2382, London, 1962.

Royal Commission on Civil Liability and Compensation for Personal Injury, *Report* (Pearson Report)(1978), HMSO, Cmnd 7054, London.

P.D.G. Skegg, ' "Informed Consent" to medical procedures', *Medicine, Science and Law*, 15, No. 2 (1975), pp. 124-30.

Colin J.H. Thomson, 'Informed consent to medical treatment in the United States', *Medical Journal of Australia*, 2 (1979), pp. 412-15.

5. Randomised controlled clinical trials

D.G. Altman, 'Statistics and ethics in medical research' in: S.M. Gore and D.G. Altman (eds), *Statistics in Practice*, British Medical Association, London (1982), pp. 1-24.

A. Bradford Hill, 'Medical ethics and controlled trials', *British Medical Journal*, ii (1963), pp. 1043-49.

David P. Byar et al., 'Randomized clinical trials: perspectives on some recent ideas', *New England Journal of Medicine*, 295 (1976), pp. 74–80.

A.L. Cochrane, *Effectiveness and Efficiency*, London, 1972.

H.A.F. Dudley, 'The controlled clinical trial and the advance of reliable knowledge: an outsider looks in', *British Medical Journal*, 287 (1983), pp. 957-60.

John F. Forbes, 'Highlights in development of randomised clinical trials', *Medical Journal of Australia* (1981), pp. 159-60.

P.D. Oldham, *Measurement in Medicine* (chapter 7), The English Universities Press, 1968.

Milton C. Weinstein, 'Allocation of subjects in medical experiments', *New England Journal of Medicine*, 291 (1974), pp. 1278-85.

6. Trials on trial

M. Baum, R. Kay and H. Scheurlen (eds), *Clinical Trials in Early Breast Cancer*, 2nd Heidelberg Symposium, Heidelberg, 14-17 December 1981, Birhauser Verlag, Germany.

M. Baum, 'Clinical trials for early breast cancer – where do we go next?', *World Medicine*, 6 February 1982.

Sissela Bok, 'The Ethics of Giving Placebos', *Scientific American*, 231 (1974), pp. 17-23.

R. Burkhardt and G. Keinle, 'Controlled clinical trials and medical ethics', *Lancet*, 2 (1978), pp. 1356-59.

R. Burkhardt and G. Keinle, 'Basic problems in controlled trials', *Journal of Medical Ethics*, 9 (1983), pp. 80-84.

A. Byer, 'The practical and ethical defects of surgical randomised prospective trials', *Journal of Medical Ethics*, 9 (1983), pp. 90-93.

T.C. Chalmers, J.B. Block and S. Lee, 'Controlled studies in clinical research', *New England Journal of Medicine*, 287 (1972), pp. 75-78.

Susan S. Ellenberg, 'Randomization designs in comparative clinical trials', *New England Journal of Medicine*, 310 (1984), pp. 1404-08.

P.A. Freund, 'Ethical problems in human experimentation', *New England Journal of Medicine*, 273 (1965), pp. 687-92.

P. Meier, 'Terminating a trial – the ethical problem', *Pharmacology and*

Therapeutics, 25 (1979), pp. 633-40.

A. Schafer, 'The ethics of the randomized clinical trial', *New England Journal of Medicine*, 307 (1982), pp. 719-24.

Beth Simmons, 'Problems in deceptive medical procedures: an ethical and legal analysis of the administration of placebos', *Journal of Medical Ethics*, 4 (1978), pp. 172-81.

D.W. Vere, 'Controlled clinical trials: the current ethical debate', *Journal of the Royal Society of Medicine*, 74 (1981), pp. 85-87.

D.W. Vere, 'Problems in controlled trials – a critical response', *Journal of Medical Ethics*, 9 (1983), pp. 85-89.

7. In whose hands?

P. Allen and W.E. Waters, 'Attitudes to research ethical committees', *Journal of Medical Ethics*, 9 (1983), pp. 61-65.

H.K. Beecher, 'Ethics and Clinical Research', *New England Journal of Medicine*, 274 (1966), pp. 1354-60.

British Medical Association, 'Local ethical committees', *British Medical Journal*, 282 (1981), p. 1010.

M.J. Denham, A. Foster and D.A.J. Tyrrell, 'Work of a district ethical committee', *British Medical Journal*, 2 (1979), pp. 1042-45.

G. Dworkin, 'Legality of consent to nontherapeutic medical research on infants and young children', *Archives of Disease in Childhood*, 53 (1978), pp. 443-46.

Ethical Committee, University College Hospital, 'Experience at a clinical research ethical review committee', *British Medical Journal*, 283 (1981), pp. 1312-14.

L.O. Gostin, 'Observations on consent to treatment and review of clinical judgement in psychiatry: a discussion paper', *Journal of the Royal Society of Medicine*, 74 (1981), pp. 742-51.

M.H. Pappworth, 'Medical ethical committees, a review of their functions', *World Medicine*, 22 February 1978.

P.D.G. Skegg, 'English law relating to experimentation on children', *Lancet*, 2 (1977), pp. 754-55.

R.N. Smith, 'Safeguards for healthy volunteers in drug studies', *Lancet*, 1 (1975), pp. 449-50.

D.W. Vere, 'Testing new drugs – the human volunteer', *Journal of Medical Ethics*, 4 (1978), pp. 81-83.

Working Party on Ethics of Research in Children, 'Guidelines to aid ethical committees considering research involving children', *British Medical Journal*, (1980), pp. 229-31.

8. Dilemmas for doctors

Marcia Angell, 'Patients' preferences in randomized clinical trials', *New*

England Journal of Medicine, 310 (1984), pp. 1385-87.

Brian P. Bliss and Alan G. Johnson, *Aims and Motives in Clinical Medicine,* London, 1975.

Thurstan B. Brewin, 'The cancer patient: communication and morale', *British Medical Journal,* 2 (1977), pp. 1623-27.

Barrie R. Cassileth, Robert V. Zupkis, Katherine Sutton-Smith and Vicki March, 'Informed consent – why are its goals imperfectly realised?', *New England Journal of Medicine,* 302 (1980), pp. 896-900.

J.C. Garnham, 'Some observations on informed consent in non-therapeutic research', *Journal of Medical Ethics,* 1 (1975), pp. 138-45.

Lawrence Goldie, 'The ethics of telling the patient', *Journal of Medical Ethics,* 8 (1982), pp. 128-33.

Nigel Kemp, Elizabeth Skinner and Jane Toms, 'Randomized clinical trials of cancer treatment – a public opinion survey', *Clinical Oncology,* 10 (1984), pp. 155–61.

Wendy S. Schain, 'Patients' rights in decision making: the case for personalism versus paternalism in health care', *Cancer,* 46 (1980), pp. 1035-41.

Kathryn M. Taylor, Richard G. Margolese and Colin L. Soskolne, 'Physicians' reasons for not entering eligible patients in a randomized clinical trial of surgery for breast cancer', *New England Journal of Medicine,* 310 (1984), pp. 1363-67.

James M. Vaccarino, 'Consent, informed consent and the consent form', *New England Journal of Medicine,* 298 (1978), p. 455.

9. Whose body is it?

John Heron and Peter Reason, 'New paradigm research and holistic medicine', *British Journal of Holistic Medicine,* 1 (1984), pp. 86-91.

Michael Young, 'Empiric Oath for Patients', *Self Health,* Journal of the College of Health, Issue 1, 1983.

Select bibliography

Henry K. Beecher, *Research and the Individual, Human Studies*, Boston, 1970.

Sissela Bok, *Lying: Moral Choice in Public and Private Life*, Quartet, London, 1980.

Sissela Bok, *Secrecy*, Oxford, 1984.

Boston Women's Health Collective, *Our Bodies, Ourselves*, Penguin, London, 1978.

The Brighton Women & Science Group, *Alice Through The Microscope*, Virago, London, 1980.

Vernon Coleman, *The Paper Doctors*, M. Temple-Smith, London, 1977.

Norman Cousins, *Anatomy of an Illness*, Bantam Books, UK, 1981.

Rene Dubos, *Mirage of Health*, Harper & Row, New York, 1959.

A.S. Duncan, G.R. Dunstan, R.B. Welbourn (eds), *Dictionary of Medical Ethics*, Darton Longman & Todd, London, 1981.

G.R. Dunstan & Mary J. Seller (eds), *Consent in Medicine*, King Edward's Hospital Fund for London, London, 1983.

Terence Dusquesne and Julian Reeves, *A Handbook of Psychoactive Medicines*, Quartet, London, 1982.

Barbara Ehrenreich and Deirdre English, *For Her Own Good*, Pluto Press, London, 1979.

Charles Fried, *Medical Experimentation: Personal Integrity and Social Policy*, Oxford, 1974.

Jory Graham, *In the Company of Others*, Gollancz, London, 1983.

Hastings Center Reports are published bi-monthly and are devoted to discussions of ethical problems of the biomedical, behavioural and social sciences. The Hastings Center, 360 Broadway, Hastings-on-Hudson, N.Y. 10706. Annual subscription $29.

Ian Kennedy, *The Unmasking of Medicine*, Allen & Unwin, London, 1981.

Ivan Illich, *Limits to Medicine*, Boyars, London, 1976.

Thomas McKeown, *The Role of Medicine – Dream, Mirage or Nemesis?*, Basil Blackwell, Oxford, 1979.

Peter Medawar, *The Art of the Soluble*, Methuen, London, 1967.

Jeanette Mitchell, *What Is To be Done About Illness and Health?*, Penguin, London, 1984.

Maurice Pappworth, *Human Guinea Pigs*, Routledge & Kegan Paul, London, 1967.

Paul Ramsey, *The Patient as Person, Explorations in Medical Ethics*, New Haven, 1970.

Russell Scott, *The Body as Property*, Viking Press, 1981.

Lewis Thomas, *The Youngest Science*, Oxford, 1984.

Peter Townsend and Nick Davidson, *Inequalities in Health: The Black Report*, Penguin, London, 1982.

A Patients' Guide to the National Health Service, Consumers' Association, 14 Buckingham Street, London WC2.

Patients' Rights, National Consumer Council, 18 Queen Anne's Gate, London SW1.

Index

abortion, 17, 19, 46, 91, 130, 136
adjuvant treatment, 77, 79
aetiology, 28, 62, 133
aged, 5, 18, 31, 39, 40, 42, 104, 124
Alliluyeva, Svetlana, 44
American Hospital Association, 125, 137–9
American Medical Association, 45
animals, experiments on, 62, 68, 95, 96, 105, 132, 133, 134
antibiotics, 63, 90
armed forces see servicemen
arthritis, 40, 77, 102, 103
Asian women in Brent, 100
assault, 115, 123, 127
Association of the British Pharmaceutical Industry (ABPI), 102, 106
Australia, clinical trials in, 84
autonomy, principle of, 5, 13, 14, 16, 18, 19, 21, 22, 23–5, 27, 30, 37, 39, 42–3, 53, 71, 78, 91, 109, 111, 119, 127, 128, 134

Barnes, Dame Josephine, 122
Bathhurst, Christopher, 122
battery, 21–2, 53, 54
Beaumont, William, 45, 46
Beecher, Henry K., 75, 86, 90, 96, 104, 127
Belmont Report (US, 1978), 52
beneficence, principle of, 28–30, 36
benefits see treatment, risks and benefits of
Bernard, Claude, 45, 46
Bill of Rights for Patients (US, 1973), 46, 125, 137–9
biomedical technology see medical technology
Bliss, Brian P., 95
blood-letting, 63
blood pressure, high see hypertension
blood samples, 126
Bok, Sissela, 25, 90, 107

Bolam v. *Friern Hospital Management Committee*, 1957, 40–1, 53
Boston Women's Health Collective, 16
bowel cancer, 9–10
breast cancer, 13, 14, 29, 30, 65, 79–84, 86–7, 98, 113, 117
Brent Health Authority, 100
Brewin, Thurston B., 116
British Medical Association (BMA), 45, 51–2, 56, 96, 97, 99, 102, 103, 122, 136
British Medical Journal, 88
Browne-Wilkinson, Lord Justice, 55

calcium deficiency, 100
Canada, informed consent in, 12, 14, 55, 56
cancer, 20, 22, 29, 31, 34, 38, 40, 64, 68, 77, 84, 105, 123
    bowel, 9–10
    breast, 13, 14, 29, 30, 65, 79–84, 86–7, 98, 113, 117
    cervical, 19, 64
    prostate, 98
    stomach, 10
Canterbury v. *Spence*, Federal Republic, 1972, 13
cervical screening, 19, 64
charities, 101, 103
Charterhouse Research Unit, 105
Chatterton v. *Gerson*, 1980, 53–4
chemotherapy, 40
childbirth, 19, 20, 62
    see also post-natal depression
children, 30, 31, 140
    in clinical trials, 42, 49, 104, 135
    handicapped, 18, 41–2, 92,

100, 103
    in hospital, 19
    proxy consent for, 39, 40
Clarke, Kenneth, 122–3
class discrimination, 5, 18–19, 35, 52, 124, 131
clinical death, 17
clinical trials, 1, 2, 3, 6, 12, 35, 47–52, 65–6, 78, 95, 101–6, 113–14
    analysis of results, 67, 73, 135
    'blind' and 'double blind', 69, 90, 91, 93
    compensation, 105, 106, 126
    concealed, 9, 10–11, 35, 43, 56–7, 64, 78–85, 90–3, 111–12
    consent, 9, 10–11, 21, 30, 35, 38, 42, 43, 47–9, 50–2, 69, 75–6, 77–84, 89, 90, 91, 98, 106, 113–16, 118, 125, 126–7, 135, 136, 138, 141–2
    controlled, 48, 51, 56–7, 63, 66, 77, 92, 100, 126, 135
    inducements, 49, 86, 102, 105–6, 132, 142
    monitoring, 9, 40, 43, 66
    multi-centre, 68, 89, 92
    non-therapeutic, 42, 48, 49, 50, 51, 65–6, 95, 104, 105, 133, 136
    null hypothesis, 70, 71
    pilot studies, 67
    protocol, 9, 43, 48, 49, 67, 68, 69, 80, 82, 83, 90, 127, 134, 135, 136
    randomised controlled trials (RCTs), 3, 9, 10–11, 38, 43, 52, 61–74, 75–94, 98–9, 109, 112, 116–17
    sample, 3, 63, 64, 67, 68, 69, 70, 80–6, 104–6

'significant difference', 70, 73
therapeutic, 48, 50–1, 66, 133
see also ethical committees; independent committees *and* placebos
Cochrane, Dr Archibald, 63–4
codes of practice, 12, 44, 45, 46–57, 66, 69, 95, 96, 102, 125–6, 130–40
Coleman, Vernon, 99, 103
Committee on the Safety of Medicines (CSM), 103, 122
Community Health Councils, 19, 46
complaints procedures, 46, 103, 125–6, 140
computerisation, 3, 69, 71, 80
concentration camps, 12, 46, 96
confidentiality, 3, 18, 26, 27, 85, 120, 131, 138, 139–40, 141–2
consent *see* informed consent
consumer movement, 19
contraception, 19, 20, 91, 121–3
Corber, Professor John, 92
Crossman, Richard, 121
Cruelty to Animals Act (1876), 96
Culver, Charles M., 41

Data Protection Bill, 3
death, 17, 118, 119, 132, 133, 136, 140
see also euthanasia
decision-making, 1–5, 10–15, 18, 19, 20, 21, 22–31, 43, 47, 53–6, 78, 80, 82–3, 89, 91, 98, 111, 112, 120, 121, 127, 128, 132
competence to decide, 34–9, 48, 55, 75–6
incompetence to decide, 39–43, 48, 111
see also voluntariness and volunteers
defensive medicine, 15, 56
deontology, 16
Depo-Provera, 121–3
depression, 5, 20, 28
post-natal, 19
DHSS, 31, 86–7, 96, 97, 122
diagnosis, 5, 46, 125, 133, 137, 139
Dictionary of Medical Ethics, 11, 81
disinfectants, 62
doctor-patient relationship *see* patient-doctor relationship
Donaldson, Sir John, 55, 56
drug companies, 101–6, 122
drugs:
consenting to, 53, 122
dependence on, 90
marketing, 101, 103
to modify behaviour, 41
monitoring, 9, 40, 43, 102, 103, 123
overdoses of, 39
side effects of, 20, 29, 38, 68, 73, 77, 91, 92, 98, 101–6, 115, 122–3
trials, 9, 40, 43, 64, 66, 69, 76–7, 90, 91, 98, 101–6, 122–3
understanding, 34, 38, 122–3
Drug Watch, 103
Dunn, Lord Justice, 55–6
Durham, Mike, 100

education, health *see* health education
electro-convulsive therapy (ECT), 40–1

embryos, research on, 2,
17–18, 50, 92, 100
see also abortion; surrogate
motherhood *and* test-tube
babies
epidemiology, 28, 62
ethical committees, 9, 35, 68,
75, 80, 94, 95–100, 101, 102,
103, 104, 105, 115
European Charter on the
Rights of Patients,
Resolution on a (1985), 46,
125–6, 139–40
European Parliament, 46,
125–6, 140
euthanasia, 17, 42
experiments:
on animals, 62, 68, 95, 96,
105, 132, 133, 134
on humans, 12, 45, 46–52,
62, 65–7, 95, 105–6, 131–3
see also clinical trials

Fisher, Sir Ronald, 63, 72
France:
health service, 124
human rights, 17

General Medical Council
(GMC), 52, 97
genetic engineering, 17
see also embryos, research
on
Geneva, Declaration of (1968),
44, 45, 95, 131, 133
geriatrics *see* aged
Germany, health service, 124
Gert, Bernard, 41
Goldzeiher, Dr, 91
government policy, 20, 30–1,
50, 95, 96, 101, 103, 105–6
see also DHSS *and* National
Health Service

GPs,4–5, 46, 68, 97, 99, 102,
104, 118
Graham, Jory, 9
grief, suppressing, 28

Halstead operation for breast
cancer, 65
Hamblin, Terry, 100
Handbook of Medical Ethics
(BMA), 51, 97, 136
Harvey, William, 62
Hawaii, Declaration of (1977),
136
health education, 20, 31
Health Research Council, 101
health rights, 17–31
see also legal rights
health services *see* National
Health Service
heart disease and surgery, 38,
89, 106
Helsinki, Declaration of (1964,
rev. 1975), 47, 48–51, 66,
69, 96, 102, 133–6
Heseltine, Michael, 105–6
Hill, Sir Austin Bradford, 61, 63
Hippocrates and the
Hippocratic Oath, 22, 28,
30, 44, 61, 95, 130–1
historical (retrospective) trials,
73, 76
Holland, breast cancer
screening, 87
Holtom, Peter, 10, 12
Home Office, 95, 96
hospitals, 4, 5, 19, 36, 104, 110,
118, 123–4, 126, 138, 139
human rights, 13, 16, 17, 21,
53, 125, 126
see also autonomy; health
rights *and* legal rights
Hurley, Professor Rosalind,
122

hypertension, 64, 102
hysterectomy, 20, 38, 125

iatrogenic diseases, 101–2
impotence, 73, 98
in vitro fertilisation *see* test-
    tube babies
independent committees,
    48–9, 50, 134, 136
infertility services and
    research, 50
information:
    communicating, 5, 11–12,
        25, 29, 34–9, 52, 69, 83,
        98, 112–17
    dishonest, 10, 25, 26–7, 90,
        111, 118–20
    eliciting, 5, 10, 35–6, 38, 110
    right not to receive, 5,
        10–11, 22, 25, 38, 39,
        111, 113, 114–15, 120
    right to receive, 10–11, 13–14,
        19, 20, 23, 33–9, 47, 53–5,
        69, 73, 75–6, 79–82, 87, 91,
        92, 110–17, 120, 125, 128,
        132, 137, 139
    understanding, 11, 22, 34–9,
        40, 41, 77, 106, 113, 118,
        132, 137
    withholding, 5, 10, 13–15,
        25–7, 33–5, 40–1, 53–7,
        76, 78–86, 90, 111–17, 137
    see also confidentiality
informed consent, concept of
    defined, 1–4, 11, 32–5
Ingelfinger, F.J., 36, 37
International Code of Medical
    Ethics, 133

Jenkins, Peter, 121
Johnson, Alan G., 95
justice, principle of, 27, 119

Kant, Immanuel, 7, 21, 23
Kennedy, Ian, 45–6
Keynes, Sir Geoffrey, 65
Kuhse, Helga, 42

laminectomy, 13
Lancet, 88, 114
lay members, of independent
    and ethical committees, 49,
    50, 97, 99, 103
legal action, 9, 10, 11, 12,
    13–15, 21–2, 40–1, 42, 53–6,
    104, 115
    compensation, 54–6, 105,
        106, 126
    expert witnesses, 54
legal rights, 21, 38, 104, 125,
    126, 137, 140
    see also human rights
'Life' organisation, 42
local ethical committees *see*
    ethical committees
Louis, Professor Pierre-
    Charles-Alexandre, 63
lumpectomy, 79–84

Macara, Dr, 97
malpractice, 9, 53, 56, 115
    see also assault; battery *and*
        negligence
mastectomy, 65, 79–84
media, the, 10, 18, 20, 31, 100,
    102
medical profession, self-
    regulation, 44, 45–6, 47, 51,
    54–6, 96, 99, 100–1, 103
medical records, 18, 26, 125,
    139, 140
medical research, 30, 42, 43,
    46–52, 65, 96–106
    funds for, 101, 105
    see also clinical trials *and*
        experiments

Medical Research Council (MRC), 50–1, 92, 97
medical technology, 2, 18, 20, 22, 50, 110, 124
menopause, 20
mental health, 28–9
Mental Health (Amendment) Act (1982), 41
mentally handicapped, 18, 39, 49, 104
mentally ill, 28–9, 37, 40, 104, 135, 140
moral rights *see* human rights

Natanson v. *Kline*, Kansas, 1960, 13
National Commission for the Protection of Human Subjects of Biomedical and Behavioral Research (US), 52
National Health Service (NHS), 18–19, 20, 30, 51, 63, 101, 124–5
nausea, 73
Nazi war criminals, 12, 46, 96
negligence, 12, 21–2, 30, 40–1, 53–6
neuro-surgery, 55–6
non-maleficence, principle of, 30, 44, 45, 47, 88
Nuremberg Code, 12, 46–8, 131–3
Nuremberg War Crimes Tribunal, 12, 46, 96

old people *see* aged
Ombudsman, 46
operations *see* surgery
Opren, 103
orchidectomy, 98
organ transplants, 17, 106
Orwell, George, 32

Oslo, Declaration of (1970), 136
Osmosin, 103

Pappworth, Maurice H., 78, 96, 99, 104
Parliament, 3, 46, 126
paternalism, 4–5, 19, 29, 36, 41, 54, 56, 111, 117–20
patient-doctor relationship, 22–31, 33, 34–43, 44–5, 51, 56, 71, 75, 76, 86, 91, 93, 110–20, 126–8, 136, 137
'patient-friends', 115
Pediatric Association, 104
Percival, Thomas, 44–5
pharmaceutical industry *see* drug companies
physically handicapped, 31
Pill, the, 20, 91
placebos, 69, 89–93, 118, 141
Porton Down, 105–6
post-natal depression, 19
pregnancy, clinical trials during, 92, 100
Pregnavite Forte F, 92
premenstrual tension, 19
press, 10, 20, 100
pressure groups, 19–20, 46, 103, 122–3
prisoners:
  in clinical trials, 49, 106
  punishment and torture of, 136
private medicine, 125
prognosis, 10, 38, 115, 118, 125, 137, 139
prostate, cancer of the, 98
proxy consent *see* treatment, proxy consent to
psychiatric treatment, 40–1, 124, 136
psychological factors, 66, 71, 74, 78, 83, 89, 110

psychosurgery, 41
puerperal fever, 62
Puxon, Dr Margaret, 123–4

radiotherapy, 13, 25, 64, 65,
   77, 79, 89
Ramsey, Paul, 27, 39, 106,
   109, 117
randomised controlled trials
   (RCTs) *see* clinical trials
Regina v. *Leonard John Henry
   Arthur*, 1981, 42
Reibl v. *Hughes*, Canada, 1980,
   55
research *see* medical research
research ethical committees *see*
   ethical committees
resource allocation, 18, 27,
   30–1, 87, 124–5
'respect for persons', 25
retrospective trials *see*
   historical trials
rheumatoid arthritis, 77
right to know *see* information,
   right to receive
risk/benefit equation *see*
   treatment, risks and benefits
   of
Royal Colleges, 52, 96–7, 102
Russell, Bertrand, 64

St Bartholomew's Hospital,
   105
San Antonio, Texas, research
   on the Pill in, 91
screening, 64
   for breast cancer, 30, 86–7
   cervical, 19, 64
sedation, 28
self-determination, right of *see*
   autonomy, principle of
self-help groups, 20
Semmelweiss, Ignaz, 62

servicemen in clinical trials,
   105–6
sex offenders, 41
sexual discrimination, 4–5, 17,
   19–20, 21, 81–2
Shaw, George Bernard, 124
Sidaway v. *the Board of
   Governors of Bethlem Royal
   Hospital*, 1984, 55–6
spina bifida, 92
Squibb, E.R. & Son, 106
statistics and statisticians, 63,
   67, 70, 72, 73, 76, 92, 94, 116
Steptoe, Patrick, 18
sterilisation, 46
stomach cancer, 10
Streptomycin, 63
stroke, 20, 39
students in clinical trials, 105,
   106
suicide attempts, 39–40
surgery, 11, 20, 29, 38, 64, 69,
   77, 79–83, 90
   consent to, 10, 11, 12, 13,
      33–4, 53–6, 80
   heart, 38, 106
   hip replacement, 125
   hysterectomy, 20, 38, 125
   laminectomy, 13
   lumpectomy, 79–84
   mastectomy, 65, 79–84
   neuro-surgery, 55–6
   orchidectomy, 98
   organ transplants, 17, 106
   psychosurgery, 41
   sterilisation, 46
surrogate motherhood, 2, 50
Sweden:
   breast cancer screening, 87
   health service, 124
Sydney, Declaration of (1968),
   136

technological advance, 2, 18, 20, 22, 50, 110, 124
television, 10, 18, 20
test-tube babies (*in vitro* fertilisation), 17, 18, 50, 106
Thalidomide, 103
'therapeutic privilege', 35, 49, 115
therapy *see* treatment
Third World, use of Depo-Provera in the, 122–3
Tokyo, Declaration of (1975), 136
treatment:
  adjuvant, 77, 79
  alternative, 1, 13, 14, 20, 33–4, 38, 64, 66, 80–1, 93, 98, 112, 116–17, 118, 138, 141
  choice of, 23, 26, 28–9, 32, 33–4, 51, 55, 64, 68, 69, 79–82, 98, 112, 118, 122, 125
  monitoring, 9, 40, 43, 66, 95
  proxy consent to, 39–43, 48, 104, 135
  right to refuse, 2, 10, 12–13, 22, 29, 32, 33, 38–9, 40–1, 43, 53, 68, 69, 77–8, 80, 82–3, 84, 104, 123–4, 125, 135, 138
  risks and benefits of, 1, 30, 38, 40–1, 42, 47, 53–4, 55, 69, 77, 81, 88, 98, 103, 104, 106, 115, 122, 132, 134–5, 141
  see also clinical trials; drugs *and* surgery
truth *see* veracity, principle of
tuberculosis, 63

unemployed in clinical trials, 105

United States:
  defensive medicine, 17, 56
  health care, 65, 124
  human rights, 16, 17, 45, 46, 125
  informed consent, 12–15, 52, 53, 54, 86, 115, 125
  research, 52, 87, 89, 91, 96, 104
University Grants Committee, 101
Upjohn, 122
urine samples, 126
utilitarianism, 16–17

vaginal examinations, 123–4, 126
valium, 5
veracity, principle of, 25–7, 119
vitamins, 90, 92, 100
voluntariness and volunteers, 32, 33–4, 43, 47, 48, 49, 66, 96, 103, 105, 132, 136

Walden, Brian, 121
Warnock Committee Report (1984), 50, 59
Whittington, Dr Richard, 9
Wigley, Mrs Margaret, 9, 43
Williams v. *Menehan*, Kansas, 1963, 13
women, sexual prejudice against *see* sexual discrimination
women's movement, 19
World Medical Association, 44, 45, 47, 133, 134, 136
World Medicine, 88–9, 100, 123

X-rays, 86, 90

Zelen, Dr Marvin, 84–6